Conflict, communism and fascism

Europe 1890–1945

Frank McDonough

CAMBRIDGE
UNIVERSITY PRESS

In memory of Irene (Rene) Kent

PUBLISHED BY THE PRESS SYNDICATE OF THE UNIVERSITY OF CAMBRIDGE
The Pitt Building, Trumpington Street, Cambridge, United Kingdom

CAMBRIDGE UNIVERSITY PRESS
The Edinburgh Building, Cambridge CB2 2RU, UK
40 West 20th Street, New York, NY 10011-4211, USA
10 Stamford Road, Oakleigh, VIC 3166, Australia
Ruiz de Alarcón 13, 28014 Madrid, Spain
Dock House, The Waterfront, Cape Town 8001, South Africa

http://www.cambridge.org

First published 2001
Reprinted 2001

Printed in the United Kingdom at the University Press, Cambridge

Typeface 10.5pt Minion   *System* QuarkXPress®

A catalogue record for this book is available from the British Library

ISBN 0 521 77796 8   paperback

Text design by Newton Harris Design Partnership

Map artwork by Kathy Baxendale

The cover shows a painting of Vladimir Ilyich Lenin (1870–1924) addressing the Red Army of Workers on 5 May 1920 (oil on canvas), painted by Isaak Izrailovich Brodsky (1883–1939) in 1933. Reproduced courtesy of Private Collection/Novosti/Bridgeman Art Library.

ACKNOWLEDGEMENTS
AKG London: pp. 4, 6*l*, 21, 33, 43, 46, 70, 87, 93, 98, 99, 107, 111; Will Dyson/Daily Herald: Centre for the Study of Cartoons and Caricature, University of Kent, Canterbury: p. 59; David Low/ Evening Standard: Centre for the Study of Cartoons and Carica-ture, University of Kent, Canterbury: pp. 62, 78, 110; Hulton Getty Picture Collection: pp. 23, 27, 41, 54, 74, 84; David King Collection: pp. 6*r*, 7, 9, 13, 17, 124; NOVOSTI (London): pp. 5, 16; Popperfoto: pp. 45, 119; Scherl/SV Bilderdienst: p. 97.

We are grateful to the University of Exeter Press for permission to reproduce extracts from *Nazism 1919–1945*, volume 4: *The German home front in World War II*, ed. J. Noakes and G. Pridham.

Every effort has been made to reach copyright holders. The pub-lisher would be pleased to hear from anyone whose rights have been unwittingly infringed.

Picture Research by Sandie Huskinson-Rolfe of PHOTOSEEKERS.

Contents

Introduction

This book examines the major events of European history from 1890 to 1945. It is primarily concerned with the main political developments of this period, but it also describes important social and economic changes. It is a period of European history which is studied by more students than any other, and it is not difficult to see why.

The period 1890–1945 saw such momentous events as the Russian Revolution and the two world wars of 1914–18 and 1939–45, which had major economic, social and political consequences for the whole of Europe. It was also a period which saw the rise and fall of Hitler's Nazi Germany and Mussolini's Fascist Italy.

The book concentrates on three of the central themes of European history in this period: the conflict which produced the two world wars, the communism which led to the Russian Revolution, and the rise and fall of fascism in Germany and Italy.

The text is organised in a broadly chronological manner, but each chapter, which contains focus and summary questions and provides an overview of key issues and events, can be treated as a self-contained study and examination topic.

Chapter 1 examines the dramatic events which led to the Russian Revolution of 1917. In Chapter 2, the origins of the First World War are fully evaluated. Chapters 3 and 4 examine the events and aftermath of the First World War. Chapter 5 examines the rise and fall of fascism in Italy from 1919 to 1945. Chapters 6 and 7 focus on Weimar Germany and the rise of Adolf Hitler, while Chapter 7 goes on to look at the origins of the Second World War. Finally, a document study focuses on the domestic policies of Nazi Germany.

The book aims to stimulate you in your study and help you to formulate your own thoughts and ideas on this fascinating period of European history.

1 Russia: the road to revolution, 1890–1917

Significant dates

1892	Witte is appointed minister of finance and embarks on a programme of industrialisation
1894	Nicholas II becomes tsar, following the death of Alexander III
1904	*February* War with Japan begins
1905	*January* 'Bloody Sunday' massacre of protesters against the tsar provokes 'revolutionary' upheaval in Russia
	August Tsar promises democratic constitution and elections
	September War with Japan ends with Japanese victory
	October Tsar issues October manifesto
1906	*May* First duma (parliament) meets (dissolved after 72 days)
	October Stolypin introduces the first agrarian reforms
1907	*March* Second duma meets (dissolved after four months)
	November Third duma meets (elected under restricted franchise and lasts until 1912)
1911	Stolypin is assassinated by a terrorist
1912	Fourth duma meets (lasts until 1917)
1914	Germany declares war on Russia
1917	*February* Strikes and civil unrest in major cities
	March Nicholas II abdicates
	April Lenin returns from exile to proclaim his April Theses, which promise 'peace, bread and land'
	July Widespread demonstrations against the provisional government (the July Days) are put down and Bolshevik leaders are jailed or forced to flee abroad

August Kornilov 'coup' is defeated but the popularity of the provisional government plummets
September Bolsheviks gain a majority in the Petrograd Soviet
October Bolsheviks seize power; Lenin becomes leader of the new communist state

Overview

In 1890, Russia, the largest state in Europe, was economically and politically backward by the standards of western Europe. Indeed, the gap between Russia and the advanced European industrial powers and the USA was widening greatly. It was becoming clear that Russia had to catch up with the rapid industrial growth of the other great European powers or it would cease to be one itself.

The census in 1897 revealed a population of 129 million people, of whom 55 million were Russians, 22 million Ukrainians, 8 million Poles and 5 million Jews. In total, Russia contained over 100 different nationalities and languages. But while the Russians made up only 43 per cent of the population, there was no place for the other nationalities in the governing elite of the tsarist regime. The Ukrainian language, for example, which was spoken by 25 million people, was dismissed as 'jargon' by Russians. Indeed, many of the minority nationalities felt they were governed by an alien power, and some minority groups such as the Poles and the Jews were persecuted quite ruthlessly by the regime. Most of the Russian population were illiterate, poverty-stricken peasants, living on the land. Compared with Europe's other major powers, Russia, although possessing enormous untapped physical resources, was badly governed and in a very impoverished condition.

This chapter examines the history of Russia in the turbulent period 1890–1917. During this time, Russia underwent enormous economic change and revolutionary upheaval, which culminated in the fall of the tsar and the advent of the world's first communist-inspired revolution in 1917.

What circumstances led to revolutionary unrest in Russia?

The nature of tsarist rule

It was generally recognised, outside Russia, that the tsarist regime was tyrannical, inefficient and bureaucratic. Tsar Nicholas II, who ruled from 1894 to 1917, was an **unlimited monarch**, whose supreme spiritual and political power was supposedly ordained by God. He promised the Russian people when he came to power that he would preserve the principle of **autocracy**. In

An **unlimited monarch** was a ruler without any constitutional restraint from government or the people.

Autocracy describes a state governed by a single ruler with unlimited power.

Tsar Nicholas II
(1868–1917).

Serfs were peasants who paid taxes to their masters, the Russian aristocracy.

Count Sergei Witte (1849–1915) was a very important Russian politician who, while minister of finance from 1892 to 1903, was the prime mover in the industrialisation of Russia. He was sacked in 1903 when the Russian economy was in the midst of an economic depression. He was brought back into office in 1905 as prime minister and he helped to negotiate a peace settlement with Japan, following the Russo-Japanese War. However, he was forced out of office after six months and was never to hold high office again.

practice, this meant that laws were handed down from above by the tsar and administered by a clumsy, bureaucratic regime and the military and security forces at the grass roots. The regime was virtually a military police state, which simply told the people what to do and what not to do. The tsar ruled Russia as a rigid autocrat, in partnership with the ruling Romanov royal family, the nobility, hand-picked ministers, leading figures in the Orthodox Church and a large bureaucracy. Although Nicholas II wielded enormous power, he was a weak and irresolute character, obsessed by family life, and had little self-confidence. He was married to Alexandra of Hesse-Darmstadt, a German princess who had leadership ambitions of her own.

The tsarist regime greatly distrusted individual effort and freedom of speech. As a result, it was supported by a very large police force, and censorship was extremely rigid. The regime had resisted calls for democratic government. Even so, it did make some effort in the latter part of the nineteenth century to introduce limited social and political reforms, most notably the emancipation of the **serfs** in 1861 and the creation of a system of local government in 1864. However, Nicholas II refused to introduce education for the mass of the population because he believed state education merely created revolutionary agitators. It was such attitudes which ensured Russian economic and political development stagnated.

The Witte system of industrial expansion, 1890–1905

These attitudes also help to explain why the tsarist regime had consistently neglected to follow the industrial development which had been sweeping across most of Europe during the nineteenth century. However, a major change in the economic policy of Russia occurred in 1892, when the tsar (Alexander III) appointed **Sergei Witte** as minister of finance. Witte believed that Russia could not remain a major European power without rapid industrial progress. There had already been some industrial expansion, particularly in railway building after 1860, but it was only during the 1890s, under Witte, that Russia embarked on a programme of more widespread industrial expansion. However, Russia lacked a highly developed pre-industrial economic base, in particular an efficient agricultural sector, which could provide the investment and stimulus for rapid industrial growth. In Britain, for example, the Agricultural Revolution had laid the foundation in the late eighteenth century for the Industrial Revolution.

The basis of Russian industrial growth in the 1890s took place in railways and heavy industry. Russian industry was concentrated in eight major industrial regions. The basis of the Witte system was direct state intervention in key sectors of the economy. The whole industrial process in Russia was planned and executed by the state, not by the enterprise of individual business people.

Peasants at the well in a village near the River Volga, south-east Russia.

Tariffs were levied on foreign goods to limit imports. Witte also encouraged foreign investment to aid industrial expansion, which came primarily from France. Indeed, most of the new companies were owned and run by foreigners. In 1900, there were 269 foreign companies operating in Russia. Industrial modernisation did produce some impressive results. The railways expanded rapidly, the production of coal and pig iron trebled and the annual rate of economic growth in the 1890s was an impressive 8 per cent, which was higher than that of any other country in Europe. In 1900, however, only 3 million people were employed in industry, and Russian society remained overwhelmingly rural and reliant on agriculture. There were also problems, especially in developing a system of investment. Banks set interest rates at a very high level, which led to many firms going bankrupt when trade went into recession. Shares in firms, quoted on the newly established stock exchange, went up and down so fast that no new company could effectively invest for the future.

Indeed, the stimulation of industry under Witte had come not from private enterprise but from the central government. As a result, rapid industrial expansion saddled Russia with very large overseas debts, which were paid for by increased taxes on the peasantry. This produced widespread famine in farming regions. Industrialisation had not produced a new solid group of

Karl Marx (1818–83).   Lenin (1870–1924).

enterprising business people. Even more worrying was the impact of industrial growth on the farming community: peasants were forced to sell more produce in order to pay the increased taxes which financed industrialisation at a time when the population was increasing.

From 1900 to 1905 industrial expansion slowed down, and there was a run of very poor harvests which increased famine in rural areas. This also led to a growth of 'revolutionary consciousness' in the countryside and food riots became commonplace. The economic growth rate fell in this period to 1.4 per cent. As a result of the economic downturn, unemployment increased, and the growing revolutionary movement flourished in the cities. The problem was that the Witte system had attempted to create industrial expansion in Russia before any major agricultural modernisation had taken place.

Summarise the major aims of Witte's industrial reforms.

The political groups demanding change in Russia

The social and economic upheaval caused by rapid industrialisation led to peasants demanding more land, to workers calling for greater rights and to the formation of three illegal political parties which advocated political reform and revolution:

1 The Liberals, composed of members of the gentry, the professions and intellectuals, wanted to create a democratic constitutional government. The Liberals formed the Union of Liberation, which promised to bring together a wide variety of groups with the aim of creating a democratic government.

Karl Marx (1818–83) was a German philosopher who argued for an equal society led by the mass of the people. He spent a great deal of his life in exile, mostly in London. He was the godfather of communism and the greatest single ideological influence on the revolutionary groups in Russia.

2 The Social Revolutionaries (SRs), an all-Russian movement, advocated an immediate revolution, which would create a democratic system and bring about land and social reform. The SRs gained widespread support from the peasants engaged in terrorist activities against leading government figures. However, many SRs believed terrorism was counter-productive and actually encouraged the tsarist regime to become more repressive.

3 The Social Democrats, attracted by the revolutionary ideas of **Karl Marx** (see note on page 6), were the political voice of the growing urban working class in the factories. The Social Democrats favoured a revolution which would bring about an end to private property and an equal society. In 1903, the party split into two distinct factions:

- The Bolsheviks (the 'majority') were led by Vladimir Ilyich Ulyanov, better known to the world as **Lenin**, who believed the creation of a tightly disciplined elite group could provide the leadership for a 'dictatorship of the proletariat', who could lead a revolution. Lenin was the most significant revolutionary leader in Russia and wrote a number of important pamphlets and books. In 1902, in *What is to be done?*, Lenin argued that a strict and disciplined party, led by an intellectual elite, could lead the Russian people to an equal **communist** society.

- The Mensheviks (the 'minority') were led by Yuly Martov, who wanted to create a mass working-class party in which the workers would rule themselves.

Leon Trotsky inspecting Red Army troops, 1918.

Lenin (1870–1924) was born Vladimir Ilyich Ulyanov, in Simbirsk. He was the son of an upper-middle-class education official and gained a university degree in law at St Petersburg University. Lenin became deeply interested in the revolutionary ideas of Karl Marx, the German communist philosopher. He spent most of his life attempting to bring about a revolution in Russia. He became the leading figure in the Social Democratic Party, and in 1903 formed the Bolshevik Party. He was forced to spend a great deal of the period 1903–17 in exile abroad. In April 1917, Lenin returned to Russia, arriving in a sealed train at Petrograd, where he declared his April Theses, which urged the immediate seizure of power by the revolutionary parties. He led the Russian Revolution, in October 1917, and he was the first leader of the communist Soviet Union until his death in 1924.

Communism is a philosophy associated with the ideas of Karl Marx. It calls for a society in which people are judged on ability and social need and share resources in a more equal manner, through state ownership and control of the means of industrial and agricultural production.

List the main revolutionary parties and give a description of their aims.

Leon Trotsky
(1879–1940) was born
Lev Davidovitch Bronstein,
in Yanovka in the Ukraine.
He was educated in
Odessa. As a youth, he
became interested in
Marxist revolutionary ideas.
He was a member of the
Social Democratic Party,
but became a critic of
Lenin, following the split of
the party in 1903, because
of his belief that a popular
mass movement was
needed to bring about a
true revolution in Russia,
not the small elite group
which Lenin preferred.
From 1905 to 1917,
Trostky was forced into
exile, spending his time
employed as a journalist.
When he returned to
Russia in 1917, he decided
to join the Bolshevik Party
and supported Lenin's call
for a second revolution. He
played a leading role in the
planning and organisation
of the October Revolution
in 1917. Following the
death of Lenin, Trotsky
became embroiled in a
power struggle with Stalin
for the leadership of the
Communist Party. It was a
struggle which led to his
eventual expulsion from
the party in 1929. Trotsky
left Russia and became a
leading critic of Stalin's
dictatorial rule. He was
assassinated in Mexico in
1940, by a secret agent of
Stalin, who plunged an ice
pick through his head.

Another prominent member of these revolutionary groups was **Leon Trotsky**, who warned that Lenin's idea of an elite party leading a revolution would eventually pave the way for the creation of an all-powerful one-party state led by a virtual dictator. For most of the period 1903–17, Lenin, Trotsky and most of the other leading Social Democrats were forced to live in exile, due to the repressive nature of the tsarist regime, but their ideas and their influence remained strong in the underground revolutionary movement.

How and why was Nicholas II able to survive the 1905 revolution?

The Russo-Japanese War, 1904–05

It was during the year 1905 that the tsarist regime faced a rapid increase in civil protests, particularly in the major cities, which threatened to turn into a revolution. The problems of the tsarist regime intensified when the Russo-Japanese War, which began in February 1904 and lasted until September 1905, led to a succession of humiliating military and naval defeats. The Russo-Japanese War grew out of differences between Russia and Japan concerning trading and naval rights in Korea and Manchuria (north-east China). Japanese military and naval leaders wanted to gain territory in Manchuria and weaken growing Russian influence in east Asia. The diplomatic position of Japan had been greatly improved through the signing of the Anglo-Japanese Treaty in 1902. As the dispute between Japan and Russia escalated during 1903, the tsar came to believe a war with Japan, whose military and naval abilities were underestimated, might serve to divert attention from Russia's growing internal problems. At the same time, Japanese leaders were prepared to risk a war with Russia, sure in the knowledge that the most powerful imperial power in the region – Britain – would not intervene. The Japanese gained a series of spectacular naval and military victories over the beleaguered tsarist regime, including the humiliating loss of the key naval base at Port Arthur (which Russia had leased from China) in January 1905. The war with Japan created great economic strains because it severely disrupted transport, brought food shortages and greatly increased government expenditure. As a result, the popularity of the tsarist regime nose-dived following military and naval defeats by Japan.

Bloody Sunday

In January 1905, in the midst of a severe winter, a strike took place at the Putilov ironworks in **St Petersburg** over the sacking of four workers, organised by Father Georgy Gapon, a leading local union organiser. Within a matter

A still from a film reconstruction of Bloody Sunday shows the crowd beginning to flee from the disciplined line of soldiers.

of days, there was a general strike throughout St Petersburg. On 9 January 1905, a peaceful demonstration, numbering 200,000 people, marched to the Winter Palace (the tsar's residence in the capital) to present a petition. The troops of the tsar, guarding the palace, supported by the local police, were ordered by their commander to open fire on the demonstrators, which left 130 dead and 300 injured. (These are the official figures – most historians suggest that 300 died and probably 1,000 were wounded.) 'Bloody Sunday' (as it became known) was a deeply significant event. It undermined the tsarist regime, and set in motion a national agitation which became known as 'the revolution of 1905'. The tsar's claim to be the 'Little Father' of his people seemed to ring hollow in the aftermath of the bloodbath on that cold and frosty morning in St Petersburg.

In February 1905, there were extensive riots in major cities and peasant revolts in the countryside. In June 1905, the crew of the battleship *Potemkin*, based in the Black Sea, mutinied. In September 1905, another wave of strikes broke out in major cities, which paralysed the whole country. During the civil unrest which gripped Russia in 1905 the role of the new industrial urban working class was a crucial factor which forced the tsar to grant democratic reforms.

St Petersburg was the capital of Russia until 1918. After the First World War broke out in 1914, it was renamed Petrograd (and has now reverted to its original name after being called Leningrad under the communist regime). The city features many lavish palaces, notably the Winter Palace, so called because it was the traditional winter residence of the tsars.

Eisenstein's famous film of 1925, *Battleship Potemkin*, re-enacted the incident.

Even so, it is easy to exaggerate the weakness of the tsarist regime in 1905 and point to the strength of the revolutionary forces. The majority of the armed forces and the police remained steadfastly loyal to the tsar, and the mutiny on the *Potemkin* was a very isolated incident. The agitators against the tsar in 1905 were not united in their aims, with some demanding revolution at one extreme and others demanding limited constitutional reform at the other. In the countryside, the peasant revolts were fought over local issues and lacked any real co-ordination. One of the most striking features of the supposed revolution of 1905 in Russia was the lack of clear leadership among those who opposed the regime.

What event triggered the 1905 revolution?

The October manifesto

It must be stressed, therefore, that Nicholas II was urged by his leading ministers to grant some concessions to the revolutionary agitators as a stop-gap measure to dampen down the civil unrest which had gripped Russia in 1905. The most important influence on Nicholas II in the aftermath of Bloody Sunday was Witte, who was brought back into office in order to deal with the crisis. It was Witte who told the tsar that he had either to grant some democratic reform or to create a military dictatorship. The tsar accepted Witte's advice and decided to make some concessions towards democratic rule, to restore order. On 17 October 1905, the tsar issued the famous October manifesto, which promised:

1 an elected parliament (duma) with legislative powers;
2 freedom of speech and association;
3 freedom from arrest without charge and imprisonment without trial.

The tsar also promised that no law would be passed without the consent of the new duma. These concessions appeared to pave the way towards full-scale democratic government. The granting of a duma by the tsar therefore greatly disrupted the revolutionary agitators and actually weakened the growing opposition which had developed in the aftermath of Bloody Sunday. After all, it seemed that the tsar had created a constitutional monarchy in Russia, with an elected parliament and democratic elections.

However, many workers' groups refused to accept the October manifesto and set up their own workers' councils (**soviets**) in St Petersburg and Moscow, but these were quickly broken up by the army in December 1905. Even among the Liberals, there was great scepticism about the sudden conversion of the tsar towards a democratic system of government. One prominent group, the Octobrists, composed of conservative landowners loyal to the tsar, did accept the manifesto, but the Kadets, liberals who represented professionals, demanded more concessions.

The **soviet** was a council, which in Russia from 1905 to 1917 became associated with the idea of local democracy, ruled by revolutionary socialists.

How far had the tsarist government solved Russia's internal problems before 1917?

The era of the dumas, 1906–17

After 1905, therefore, the tsar embarked on his first attempt at democratic government with all the enthusiasm of a confirmed alcoholic forced to attend a temperance meeting. Even before the first duma met, Nicholas II, who had recovered his nerve somewhat, passed the Fundamental Laws in April 1906, which significantly modified the concessions offered by the October manifesto. The tsar announced under the Fundamental Laws that he was to retain most of his autocratic powers, and would have the final say over decisions of the cabinet and the armed forces, and in the field of foreign affairs. The power over the introduction of laws was shared between the duma and the newly established Council of Empire, which had a veto over the laws passed in the duma, and whose members were appointed by the tsar. It was also decided that the tsar could enact laws by decree when the duma was not in session. In essence, the concessions of the October manifesto were severely curtailed by these Fundamental Laws even before the duma had met for the first time.

The first duma, May–July 1906

The first duma lasted for less than three months. The Kadets, who were disappointed by the Fundamental Laws, were the largest grouping in the first duma. They demanded that the cabinet be made responsible to the duma, and called for reform of the Council of Empire, as well as land reforms aimed at the peasantry. The tsar rejected these demands and dissolved the duma on the grounds it had exceeded its powers.

The second duma, March–June 1907

The second duma met in March 1907, following a national election. Over 25 per cent of its members belonged to the revolutionary parties, but the extreme right-wing Conservatives also increased their vote. There were many rowdy debates during the brief and eventful period of the second duma, which Lenin described as 'the most revolutionary popular representative body in Europe, in the most backward, reactionary country'. The second duma was dissolved in June 1907, on the grounds that a Social Democratic member was plotting to assassinate the tsar (a charge which was completely false). The end of the second duma coincided with a radical change in the electoral law, which meant that only landowners and wealthy town dwellers would be allowed to vote in future elections. The tsarist regime also introduced new repressive measures against opposition parties, and severe censorship (after its suspension by the October manifesto), which led to many leading revolutionary figures either ending up in jail or being forced once more into exile abroad.

These measures showed that the tsar had not grasped that real democracy was needed in Russia or else the revolutionary alternative would remain popular.

The third ('loyal') duma, 1907–12

Elections for the third duma produced an overwhelming majority for the Octobrists, the loyal landowning supporters of the tsar. The Kadets were reduced to 54 seats and the SRs to less than 10. The third duma, which was generally loyal to the wishes of the tsar and his chief minister Peter Stolypin, lasted for its full term.

The fourth duma, 1912–17

The fourth duma was also dominated by the conservative property owners. Yet the previous harmonious relationship between the tsar and the landowning elite became increasingly strained during the period of the fourth duma. Many Russian aristocrats were concerned about the close relationship which had developed between Alexandra, the Russian empress, and the sinister **Gregory Rasputin**. Rasputin claimed he had mystical healing powers which could help the tsar's son, who suffered from the blood disorder haemophilia. He was also rumoured to be the lover of Alexandra (a rumour that was probably incorrect). The influence of the unpredictable and often drunken Rasputin over the court of Nicholas II, and particularly his close association with the tsarina, alarmed many members of the Russian aristocracy. Of even more concern to members of the duma was Rasputin's growing ability to influence the tsar in his choice of ministers and close advisers. As a consequence, the fourth duma adopted an increasingly critical attitude towards the tsar. Indeed, it was a group of Russian nobles who poisoned and then shot Rasputin in December 1916 in a vain attempt to save the reputation of the tsar from public ridicule. The tsarina mourned Rasputin, and claimed that he had only tried to save the tsarist regime.

Gregory Rasputin (1871–1916) was born in Siberia. He came from a peasant family. He described himself as a 'mystic' with healing powers; although he was popularly known as 'the mad monk', he never belonged to a monastery. Rasputin was a heavy drinker and a notorious womaniser, whose close relationship with the tsarina created a scandal in the press during the First World War. In December 1916, Rasputin was murdered by a Russian noble.

Identify the major criticisms of the tsarist regime offered by the fourth duma.

The land reforms of Stolypin, 1906–14

The failure of the duma system has led many historians to argue that Russia was already heading for revolution before the onset of war in 1914, but there are other historians who suggest that it was becoming a more modern state in this period. The land reforms of Peter Stolypin are often cited as evidence that the problems of the Russian peasants might have been solved if there had been no First World War.

Stolypin, who was prime minister from 1906 until 1911, believed the aspirations of the Russian peasants had to be satisfied in order to prevent a revolution. One particular source of unrest was the village commune, or *mir*, a self-governing community of peasant households which also had control over

A satirical cartoon of
Rasputin with the tsar and
tsarina. The artist emphasises
Rasputin's power by depicting
him as a menacing figure in
the centre of the picture.

the local farmland. A peasant's own land for cultivation was in several separate small plots. Stolypin sought to give the peasants an opportunity to leave the commune and to consolidate their land holdings as privately owned small-holdings. In this way they would be free to join the rank of the kulaks, the wealthier, landowning peasants. Political self-interest was a key motive behind Stolypin's reforms. The kulaks were generally prosperous, patriotic and loyal to the tsarist regime. In essence, Stolypin gambled on the strongly pro-tsarist farmers being able to improve agricultural efficiency. This is why he dubbed his reforms the 'Wager on the Strong'.

The impact of Stolypin's reforms varied from region to region. In the south, there was no real growth in the number of kulaks. In central Russia, the growth of industry impeded the development of a new group of kulaks. In the north, a lack of transport and the presence of heavily forested regions also meant there was little change in the existing peasant farming practices. In the western regions, however, especially in the Ukraine, the policy worked very successfully: over half of all farms were owned by kulaks. Wherever the kulak type of farm operated, there were significant improvements in agricultural productivity and efficiency.

Stolypin was assassinated in 1911, but his agricultural policies were continued after his death. Whether they would have solved the underlying problems of Russian peasants in the long term is difficult to calculate. His reforms did improve agricultural productivity. From 1908 to 1912, the grain yield rose by 20 per cent and the potato crop increased by 25 per cent. The war came at the wrong moment for the tsarist regime, as the land problem remained unresolved.

Identify the major aims of Stolypin's reforms.

The Russian economy, 1905–14

The Russian economy grew at an impressive annual rate of 6 per cent from 1905 to 1914. The government allowed private business to lead this surge of industrial growth, unlike in the 1890s when the state had been the engine room of growth. From 1908 to 1914, there was substantial growth in the coal, steel and pig iron industries. The number of industrial workers grew in the same period from 1.6 million to 2.5 million. However, the wages of industrial workers remained extremely low. The number of strikes in industry, which fell from 1905 to 1910, rose steeply between 1911 and 1914. Political discontent in the major cities still remained high.

Historical interpretation: Russia, 1905–14

The period from the 1905 revolution to the outbreak of the First World War has been the subject of intense historical debate. This has been carried on by 'optimists', who suggest that Russia was developing into a more modern democratic and industrialised state before 1914, which may have avoided revolution in the absence of the First World War, and the 'pessimists', who argue that Nicholas II had undermined the democratic reforms of 1905 and remained out of touch with the Russian people.

The pessimist school concentrates on examining the political failings of the 1905 revolution. They have suggested Nicholas II never had any intention of allowing the duma any real power within the government of Russia. The pessimists have also pointed to the sharp increase in strikes in major cities and increased repression against revolutionaries as further evidence of the anti-democratic nature of the tsarist regime from 1905 to 1914.

The optimist school of historians suggests that the democratic reforms enacted after 1905 put Russia on the road towards democracy. They have also shown how the fourth duma became increasingly critical of the rule of Nicholas II. Indeed, the optimists suggest that a gulf was opening up between the Russian nobles and the tsar which would probably have led to further democratic reforms in Russia, even in the absence of the war. In addition, the optimists suggest that Russian agriculture would have been transformed had Stolypin's reforms been allowed to continue without the disruption caused by the war.

Of course, the major problem with the whole optimist and pessimist debate over the state of Russia before 1914 is that it is centred around a 'might have been' theory. However, historians are forced to explain what actually did happen. In this respect, the impact the First World War is crucial for understanding why the tsarist regime did eventually collapse.

Why were there two revolutions in Russia in 1917?

The impact of the war

Russian involvement in the First World War proved disastrous for the tsarist regime. The impact of a highly technological style of warfare exposed the limitations of the arthritic tsarist system of government. The Russian armed forces were unprepared for war against Germany, the strongest military power in Europe. By February 1917, 6 million Russian soldiers had been killed and a further 4.2 million severely wounded. Successive military defeats led to a deterioration of morale within the army. Another major source of discontent within the army was the poor supply of equipment. In 1914, the Russian army required 18 million rifles, but was supplied with only 7 million, and there was not enough ammunition even for those guns the Russian soldiers did carry. The high casualty rates among officers led to the promotion to the officer corps of many members of the middle class who were not as loyal to the tsar as aristocratic officers.

The economic effects of the war were equally disastrous. As Russian factories moved production from consumer goods to munitions, there were severe shortages of basic goods in all the major Russian cities. The rail system did not function effectively. As the war progressed, civilian supplies were given a low priority, which added to food shortages. The economic blockade by Germany and its allies added to a miserable picture. In this gloomy climate, the peasants in the countryside went over to a subsistence economy and stopped producing a surplus for export to the cities.

Nicholas II, never fully in tune with public opinion in Russia, became even more detached from the sorry position of its soldiers at the front, and was seemingly unconcerned about the falling living standards of the civilians in the cities and the peasants in the countryside. He dealt with the growing economic crisis by printing paper roubles, which simply pushed up the prices of basic necessities even higher. The tsar also consistently rejected demands from the duma to appoint professional and technical experts to key posts in the government and the army.

Russian soldiers at the front, reading an illegal Bolshevik newspaper.

By the end of 1916, Russia was limping towards certain military defeat. Over a thousand factories were forced to close down owing to a lack of raw materials. The railway network was almost at a standstill due to shortages of coal. Many soldiers, hungry, dispirited and without even basic supplies of food and ammunition, simply gave up the hopeless struggle. Meanwhile, demonstrations and riots were breaking out in all major cities and towns. Nicholas II seemed unable to provide effective leadership during the war, and was overwhelmed by the mounting political and economic discontent which he faced from the Russian people.

Identify two major reasons why the tsarist regime collapsed.

The fall of the tsarist regime, March 1917

The end for Nicholas II came suddenly, but not unexpectedly, in March 1917. The chain of events which led to the first revolution of 1917 in Russia may have begun with a riot by 400,000 workers in Petrograd on 23 February, but it was the paralysing effects of the war, and the inability of the tsarist regime to deal with them, which had set the wheels of revolution in motion. The crisis escalated when the troops guarding the Putilov armaments factory in Petrograd not only refused to fire on the rioters, but actually joined in the demonstrations. Indeed, most of the army shared the general view that the tsar's chaotic rule should come to an abrupt end.

The mob, out on the streets, seized public buildings, even releasing prisoners from jails. On 28 February 1917, the Tauride Palace was occupied by workers, and the next day the leading ministers of the tsarist government were arrested. On 2 March 1917, Nicholas II decided to abdicate, ending over a thousand years of rule by the Romanov dynasty over Russia, on a railway platform, his train having been stopped by a noisy group of demonstrating railway workers. The tsar had fallen in a spontaneous and unplanned uprising, led by the workers in the major cities, but brought about by the intolerable strains which the First World War had placed on the decaying tsarist state. On the day Nicholas II abdicated, there was virtually no one in Russia prepared to defend the continuance of tsarist autocracy. As a result, the end of the Romanov dynasty was warmly welcomed by all the political parties and the majority of the Russian people.

The provisional government

In the view of **Alexander Kerensky**, a member of the Petrograd Soviet of Workers' and Soldiers' Deputies and a leading figure in the fall of the tsar, the February revolution 'marked the end of a long and painful trail from pure absolutism to absolute democracy'. However, the fall of the tsar produced great confusion and uncertainty about who now ruled the Russian empire, and what sort of political system would emerge from the ashes of tsarist autocracy. It was pretty clear that some form of democratic government would follow. In the beginning the only places to look for leadership were the duma, a mainly middle-class body, which had played a very minor role in the fall of the tsar, and the Petrograd Soviet, the leading revolutionary council, set up by workers, which had been the engine room of the revolt which brought about the February revolution.

A special temporary committee, consisting of the members of the duma and the Petrograd Soviet, set up a provisional government, with Prince Georgy Lvov, a Liberal, as prime minister. Indeed, a number of the members of the temporary committee actually favoured the preservation of the tsar, because they feared anarchy, perhaps even civil war, might grow out of the chaos of the February revolution.

The major aim of the provisional government was to exercise democratic power until free elections to a new constituent assembly (which would create a new constitution) took place. The new government was dominated by the Kadets, which contained liberals and conservatives from the nobility, the civil service, the army, large landowners and professionals. Most of the Kadets were unsuitable to lead a democratic government, as they would have preferred the

Alexander Kerensky (1881–1970) was born in Simbirsk and studied law. He was a member of the SRs and was a member of the duma from 1912. He played an important role in the fall of the tsar in March 1917. He was appointed minister of justice in the provisional government, and was prime minister from July, until the Bolsheviks took power. He went into exile to France after the second Russian Revolution in 1917. He then went to live in the USA.

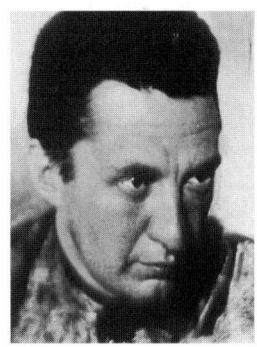

Alexander Kerensky in 1917.

continuation of some form of constitutional monarchy. The only representative of the revolutionary parties included in the provisional government was Alexander Kerensky, the minister of justice and an SR. The SRs were the most popular revolutionary grouping, with a million members, but they did not want power because they believed the revolution was only at its bourgeois stage (see below). Kerensky was a lawyer by training, and had entered the duma in 1912 as an SR. He played a leading part in rousing the opposition to the tsar in February 1917 and he was a member of the Petrograd Soviet and the provisional government. Although an SR, Kerensky was in fact middle class, liberal and democratic in his political outlook.

The other major revolutionary grouping supportive of the provisional government was the Mensheviks, who also wanted a bourgeois or middle-class group to run the new democratic government. The Menshevik Party boasted 200,000 members, drawn primarily from the industrial working class. To the Kadets, the SRs and the Mensheviks, therefore, Kerensky seemed the ideal figure to bring about a modern liberal and democratic political system in Russia.

There was to be a free press, free speech, an eight-hour day for workers, the release of all political prisoners and the abolition of the death penalty. Alongside the provisional government, local soviets were established spontaneously in a number of cities, and these challenged the authority of the new government. The soviets were dominated by the Mensheviks, the party of the industrial workers, and the SRs, the party of the peasant soldiers and farmers. In essence, a system of 'dual power' existed for most of 1917, whereby the soviets allowed the provisional government to remain in office, while at the same time retaining a sort of informal veto over any measures the new government wished to implement.

In the view of the Mensheviks and the SRs, the February revolution was a bourgeois revolution led by middle-class Liberals. The role of the workers was to allow the Liberals to rule, and thereby help to create the modern democratic society out of which would emerge a socialist stage, when the revolutionary parties would take power. This complex theory, based on an interpretation by the Mensheviks of the writings of Karl Marx, was difficult for the average Russian to understand and proved a recipe for chaos. Indeed, the Mensheviks seemed very odd revolutionaries because they were always pointing out the difficulties any socialist government would face ruling 'backward' Russia. The leaders of the Petrograd Soviet, therefore, argued that they were not ready to take power, while the provisional government argued that it could not fully exercise power until the elections for the new democratic constituent assembly took place. In the meantime, any policy of the provisional government required the support of the soviets.

The provisional government, with the agreement of the soviets, took the deeply unpopular decision to continue with the war. The SRs and the Mensheviks supported this decision because they did not want to conclude a separate peace treaty with imperial Germany, which would only lead to increased German power in eastern Europe and the possible defeat of the western 'bourgeois' Allies, Britain and France. At this time, most workers, soldiers and peasants were in favour of a swift end to hostilities. Yet a further offensive was planned by the army for the summer of 1917. The provisional government had been under great pressure from the Allies to remain in the war, even though morale and discipline in the army had virtually collapsed. The new government was also reluctant to introduce a programme of land reform, which caused great resentment among peasants in the countryside. The delay in calling the elections to the constituent assembly added to the mounting state of discontent. If elections to a new democratic assembly had been called quickly by the provisional government, there is little doubt that the SRs would have gained a massive victory. Such an election would also have exposed the limited popularity of the Bolshevik Party among the Russian population.

Give two reasons why the Mensheviks and the SRs refused to take power.

The impact of Lenin

Into this confused situation arrived the clear-sighted and decisive political figure of Lenin, the Bolshevik leader, who decided to return to Russia following his years in exile abroad. There is little doubt that Lenin's role in the momentous events of 1917 reveal that **personalities in history** do matter. The return of Lenin to Russia from Zurich, in a sealed train, was made possible only with the agreement of the German government, which granted the Russian revolutionary a free passage in the hope he would end Russia's involvement in the war. This was, perhaps, the most significant railway journey in modern history. Lenin arrived at the Finland Station (on time) in Petrograd on 3 April 1917, where he was greeted by a waiting crowd of supporters. What Lenin found on his arrival in Petrograd was a surreal situation in which the most radical revolutionaries were supporting a liberal provisional government.

Lenin quickly sensed the mood of the masses and he advocated a different approach to the revolutionary situation in Russia, which he outlined in what has become known as the April Theses. Lenin argued that the Bolshevik Party must oppose the war (to give peace a chance) and should offer no further support to the provisional government. He believed the First World War was an imperialist war and advocated a separate peace treaty with Germany to end the fighting on the eastern front. Lenin also argued that all power should pass to the soviets. At the same time, he coined the very popular Bolshevik slogan 'peace, bread and land', which seemed to express the sentiments of the ordinary

Personalities in history forms part of a debate about whether history is altered more by the actions of great leaders or more by underlying social and economic changes.

Russian citizen. Oddly enough, Lenin's apparently logical solution to the political crisis in Russia, even though it meant the acceptance of military defeat at the hands of Germany, was still not accepted by the leaders of the Mensheviks or the SRs. Even within the Bolshevik Party, Lenin's views were not immediately supported. As a result, the major impact of Lenin's April Theses was to isolate him and the Bolshevik Party from the other socialist parties, whose leaders continued to support the provisional government. However, Lenin's April Theses did gain the support of Leon Trotsky, who joined the Bolshevik Party in the summer of 1917 and who played a major role in organising opposition to the provisional government and undertaking detailed planning for the Bolshevik seizure of power in October 1917.

> Identify three aims of Lenin's April Theses.

The July Days and the Kornilov uprising

In May 1917, a new cabinet was formed, led by Kerensky, which included six SRs. Kerensky gained the agreement of the soviets to launch a new military offensive. This new offensive, in June 1917, was a complete failure and led to a collapse of morale in the army.

A number of anti-war Bolshevik demonstrations took place in early July (the July Days), beginning with a revolt by 20,000 sailors in Kronstadt, a port in northern Russia. This was followed by major demonstrations against the war in many major cities. On 4 July 1917, a mob surrounded the Tauride Palace, chanting for the leaders of the Mensheviks and the SRs to take power. These demonstrations led to the creation of a new 18-member cabinet, which included 11 socialists. However, Kerensky, realising the growing threat posed to the provisional government from the Bolsheviks, decided to order a crackdown against Lenin and his supporters. The provisional government accused Lenin of being a German agent, and he was forced to flee back into exile. Lenin travelled by train to Finland, disguised as a train driver's mate, clean-shaven and wearing a blond wig. Many other leading Bolshevik figures fled into exile, while others were arrested. This high-handed attempt to suppress the Bolshevik Party did little to weaken Lenin's popularity. Indeed, from April to July 1917 membership of the Bolshevik Party grew from 80,000 to 200,000. The failure of the July demonstrations served to convince Lenin that it would not be possible for the Bolsheviks to gain power by peaceful means: a carefully planned seizure of power was required. In other words, Lenin had abandoned his idea of giving all power to the soviets in favour of mounting an armed uprising designed to give power to the Bolshevik Party.

In August 1917, General Lavr Kornilov, the commander-in-chief of the army, decided to mount a right-wing coup, which was designed to strengthen the hold of the liberals in the provisional government. However, the Kornilov revolt was a bungled failure. Kornilov claimed that he was trying to create a

Troops firing on Bolshevik demonstrators in the streets of Petrograd in July 1917.

'strong government', but all he did was further to undermine the credibility of the provisional government. In the weeks following the Kornilov affair, there was a complete collapse of discipline in the army and a complete breakdown of law and order. The authority of the provisional government was rapidly draining away.

Briefly describe why the Kornilov revolt failed.

The Bolshevik seizure of power, October 1917

As the fortunes of the provisional government dipped, the political position of the Bolshevik Party, outlined by Lenin in his April Theses, gathered greater support within the Petrograd Soviet. The Bolsheviks were gaining control of many of the factory committees in leading industrial plants throughout Petrograd. They were also winning over many sections of the army and police leaders in the city. In September 1917, the Bolsheviks gained a majority in the Petrograd Soviet and began to press for an armed insurrection to overthrow the toothless provisional government. Lenin's promise to end the war, give land to the peasants and power to the soviets began to win over many new supporters in the major industrial areas. Kerensky appealed to the Bolshevik Party for support, and he released many party members who had been arrested during the July Days. In October 1917, Lenin urged the Bolshevik Party to seize power. The planning for the take-over of power by the Bolsheviks was left to Leon Trotsky. The provisional government heard rumours about the planning of the coup, but did not act swiftly or decisively to prevent it.

On 25 October 1917, the Congress of Soviets opened in Petrograd, with the announcement that the provisional government had been overthrown. During the same evening, Bolshevik troops seized key government buildings in Petrograd, and arrested the leading members of the provisional government. The Menshevik and SR Party leaders expressed their opposition to the Bolshevik seizure of power but, rather than attempting to challenge the right of the Bolsheviks to take office, chose to march out of the Congress, with little idea of what course of action they would now take. Leon Trotsky called after these indecisive and politically inept revolutionaries as they trooped out of the Congress: 'Go where you belong, to the dustbin of history.' This proved a very accurate prediction.

In the early hours of 26 October, the Bolsheviks had seized the Winter Palace. Lenin returned from exile to become the first leader of the Soviet Union, the first communist state in history. Lenin and the Bolsheviks had seized power in a cleverly planned coup, organised by Leon Trotsky, and mounted against a deeply unpopular provisional government, supported by a divided and muddled group of socialists. At the time the Bolsheviks seized power, their support in the Russian countryside was negligible. As a result, Lenin realised his regime would face great internal opposition before the Bolsheviks could strengthen their grip on power. Lenin promised to give land to the peasants, distribute bread to those starving, give power to the soviets and end the war. Land was given to the peasants. Russia under Lenin became a union of soviet republics (the Soviet Union). The war was ended through the Treaty of Brest-Litovsk in March 1918. The end of the war also led to better food supplies.

Yet Lenin had gained power not for the soviets but for the highly disciplined Bolshevik Party. In power, Lenin sought to increase the party's grip over Russia. Hence, Russia under the Bolsheviks developed into a one-party state led by a strong leader in charge of a powerful central government machine. Lenin called it the 'dictatorship of the proletariat'. He promised that the power of the state would eventually wither away, leaving the people in a state of equality under communism. Yet the state did not wither away. On the contrary, the power of the state grew stronger, especially after the victory of the Red Army in the Russian civil war (1918–21). The process leading to a one-party state, ruled by a single dictator, became complete during the rule of **Joseph Stalin**, who succeeded Lenin after his death in 1924.

As Soviet dictator, **Joseph Stalin** exercised power ruthlessly, using the secret police and show trials to purge political opponents. He brutally collectivised agriculture, rapidly industrialised the country and led the Soviet Union through the 'Great Patriotic War' (1941–45) into the nuclear age.

Identify two main reasons why the Bolsheviks seized power.

Stalin (1879–1953) as an underground revolutionary, from the files of the St Petersburg police, 1912–13.

Historical interpretation: the 1917 Russian Revolution

There has been enormous debate over the Russian Revolution of 1917. For E. H. Carr, the October revolution was a 'coup d'état', planned by Lenin and the Bolshevik Party, as events unfolded in 1917, which eventually destroyed all opposition groups to create a one-party state. Robert Daniels has described the Russian Revolution as a 'historical accident' which brought to power a party which lacked popular support from the peasants and the vast majority of the Russian people. According to this view, the October revolution was due to the brilliant leadership skills of Lenin, and the superb organisational abilities of Trotsky; the leaders of the Bolshevik Party were able to profit from the mistakes and blunders of the provisional government and the unwillingness of the Mensheviks and the SRs to seize power. In Marc Ferro's view, the impact of the First World War was the vital factor which led to revolution in Russia. In essence, Ferro suggests that the collapse of the tsarist regime in 1917, which was brought about largely by failure in the war, created a vacuum in Russian politics. It was out of this chaos that Lenin and the Bolshevik Party emerged. Most historians accept, therefore, that in the revolutionary situation of 1917, the outstanding political leadership of Lenin was the vital factor which ensured a second revolution took place. Indeed, the events of 1917 in Russia show how great individuals can make a decisive impact on historical events.

Summary questions

1 Identify and explain the importance of at least *two* problems which caused instability in Russia before 1914.

2 Identify and explain how Nicholas II attempted to solve at least *two* of Russia's internal problems before 1914.

3 Compare the importance of at least *three* problems which contributed to the overthrow of Nicholas II in 1917.

4 Identify and explain any *two* problems for the provisional government in 1917.

2

The origins of the First World War, 1890–1914

Focus questions

◆ Did the formation of diplomatic alignments and German 'world policy' help to cause friction in international affairs from 1890 to 1914?

◆ How did international events over 1905–14 lead up to the outbreak of war?

◆ Which nation was most to blame for the outbreak of the First World War?

Significant dates

1882	Germany, Austria-Hungary and Italy sign the Triple Alliance
1894	France and Russia agree an alliance
1904	Britain and France sign the Entente Cordiale, designed to settle Anglo-French colonial differences
1905	First Moroccan crisis
1906	*January* Algeciras conference settles Franco-German dispute over Morocco *February* Royal Navy launches new, state-of-the-art dreadnought battleship, which intensifies the Anglo-German naval race
1907	Britain and Russia sign the Anglo-Russian Convention
1908	Austria-Hungary, with the support of Germany, takes control of Bosnia-Herzegovina
1911	Second Moroccan crisis, dubbed the 'Agadir crisis', brings France and Germany to the brink of war (the crisis was resolved by an agreement whereby Germany recognised French dominance in Morocco)
1912	First Balkan War begins (results in defeat for Turkey)
1913	Second Balkan War breaks out (Greece and Serbia gain victory over their former ally Bulgaria)
1914	*28 June* Archduke Franz Ferdinand assassinated in Sarajevo by a member of a Bosnian terrorist group *23 July* Austria-Hungary (whose rulers blame Serbia for the assassination of Archduke Franz Ferdinand) issues an ultimatum to Serbia *28 July* Austria-Hungary declares war on Serbia *1 August* Germany declares war on Russia *3 August* Germany invades Belgium and declares war on France *4 August* Britain declares war on Germany

Overview

In 1890, several factors were already undermining European stability:

1 The leading European powers had participated in a fresh surge of imperialism in Africa and Asia. The 'scramble for Africa' (from 1880 to 1900) resulted in 90 per cent of African territory being under the control of five European powers: Britain, France, Germany, Italy and Belgium. The European powers had also engaged in a feverish scramble for territory in Asia, which created further divisions and areas of disagreement among them.

2 There was a growth of **nationalism** in Europe. The major powers wanted to expand, while national groups were demanding freedom from imperial rule through national self-determination. The flash-point of European nationalism was the Balkans, a region where many small nations demanded the right to rule themselves.

3 An arms race was developing between European powers, on land and at sea. The most dramatic aspect of this arms race was the Anglo-German naval race.

4 There was also a trend towards the formation of alliances and diplomatic agreements among the major powers in Europe, which eventually divided Europe into two distinct rival blocs: the Triple Alliance (Germany, Austria-Hungary and Italy) and the Triple Entente (Britain, France and Russia).

5 The growth of German power in Europe produced fear and tension in most of Germany's major rivals.

6 There was a series of diplomatic crises from 1905 to 1914, which increased tension between the major powers.

The outbreak of the First World War, therefore, was really the culmination of a long-term crisis in European affairs.

Nationalism is the strong desire for unity among a group of people, and is often expressed in pride in the characteristics and actions of a single nation or ethnic group.

Did the formation of diplomatic alignments and German 'world policy' help to cause friction in international affairs from 1890 to 1914?

The rise of Germany and its consequences

The growth of Germany produced tension in European relations. After a coalition of German states led by Prussia had defeated France in the Franco-Prussian War (1870–71), a newly unified German nation lay at the centre of Europe. Its emergence as the largest military power and a rising industrial force led to fears that Germany might attempt to disrupt the delicate **balance of power** on the continent.

These widely held fears of German aims, which were a key feature of European affairs for the whole period 1871–1914, were eased by the conciliatory

Balance of power describes the relative power of nations or groups of nations. The ideal balance of power among nations was assumed to exist when no one single power had a military or diplomatic dominance over all the others.

foreign policy followed by Otto von Bismarck, the German chancellor, from 1871 until his fall from power in 1890. Bismarck secured a dominant position for Germany in European affairs by means of a series of diplomatic agreements, the most significant being the formation of the Triple Alliance with Austria-Hungary and Italy (1882).

Bismark also tried to improve Germany's relations with Britain, France and Russia. He was the prime mover in bringing order to the 'scramble for Africa' at the Berlin West Africa Conference (1884–85). The fall of Bismarck from power in 1890, therefore, was a significant moment in European affairs because the conciliatory foreign policy he followed, which had placed Germany in a strong diplomatic position, was not continued by his successors.

Kaiser Wilhelm II and German world policy

Under Kaiser Wilhelm II, Germany adopted a bold and confrontational approach to European and colonial affairs. In 1897, for example, the kaiser announced that Germany, already in possession of Europe's largest army, would follow a 'world policy' (*Weltpolitik*), aiming to create a large German colonial empire, to build a strong navy and to use foreign policy success to strengthen the power of the monarchy over the German people.

The language used by the kaiser in pursuing what he called 'Germany's place in the sun' was confrontational, and the policy greatly contributed to increased tension in European affairs, primarily because the kaiser began to make sudden interventions in major international issues, which caused a growing fear among Germany's rivals that German ambitions extended towards a desire for European, perhaps even world, domination.

Kaiser Wilhelm II
(1859–1941).

The development of alliances

The most important consequence of Germany's world policy was that it encouraged a division of the major European powers into two powerful diplomatic and military groupings. The process began with the formation of the Triple Alliance but, while Bismarck had ruled Germany, no rival alliances had been formed. In 1894, however, France and Russia formed the Dual Alliance, which meant Germany was liable to face a European war on two fronts.

Germany's diplomatic position deteriorated further in 1904 when the British government, which had traditionally followed a policy of 'splendid isolation' from European affairs, decided to sign a diplomatic agreement with France, known as the Entente Cordiale. The Anglo-French **entente** was – on paper – a mere colonial agreement, designed to settle long-standing imperial disagreements between Britain and France, in Africa, Canada and Asia, but it encouraged the growth of close Anglo-French relations between 1904 and 1914.

Entente denotes a friendly understanding between two nations, without any military commitments to defend each other in the event of war.

In 1907, Britain signed the Anglo-Russian Convention, which brought Germany's three most powerful European rivals (Britain, France and Russia) into a much closer diplomatic friendship than had ever existed before. The diplomatic estrangement of Germany from all three of these major European powers, which the kaiser had encouraged by his own clumsy diplomacy, was certainly increasing from 1900 onwards.

Attempts to improve European relations

It would, however, be misleading to suggest all the European powers wanted war to break out. In fact, there were many attempts to improve European relations. The alliance groupings were not designed to hasten war, but to prevent it. More problems were decided by arbitration and diplomatic agreement in the period 1880–1914 than in any previous period of history. There was also a great increase in mutually dependent trade going on in Europe in the years before the outbreak of the First World War. In 1898, Tsar Nicholas II proposed an international conference to halt the growth of armies and navies in Europe. There were two major conferences held in The Hague between the European powers in 1899 and 1907 at which a permanent court of arbitration was established. It is perhaps significant that calls for reductions in arms, which were supported by Britain, Russia and France, at both Hague conferences, were flatly rejected by the German government. It is probably worth adding that in most European countries before 1914 there were strong anti-war movements, which received popular support. Hence, it is important to emphasise that war was not inevitable.

How did international events between 1905 and 1914 lead up to the outbreak of war?

The international crisis which led to war developed in a piecemeal fashion. It was intensified by a number of important events which added to the tension between the major powers and made diplomatic harmony much less easy to achieve.

The Morocco crisis of 1905–06

Morocco had until the late nineteenth century been part of the Turkish Ottoman Empire, but then increasingly came under the influence of France. Germany, which also had interests in the country, sought to challenge the French right to economic dominance in Morocco. The crisis in 1905 was a high-handed attempt by Germany to test the strength of the Anglo-French entente. In January 1905, a French diplomatic mission arrived in Fez, the capital of Morocco, aiming to gain special privileges for French traders. In a highly provocative move, the kaiser sailed on board a German battleship into Tangier, a leading Moroccan port. On arrival, the kaiser demanded equal treatment for German traders.

The German government also demanded an international conference to settle trading rights in Morocco. This move was resisted by Théophile Delcassé, the French foreign minister (who was forced to resign), but not by the French cabinet, which feared the crisis might provoke a Franco-German war, and which did agree to settle Franco-German differences over trade in Morocco at an international conference in Algeciras in Spain (which took place between January and April 1906).

Because the French had given in to the kaiser's demands for a conference, it seemed, to the German government at least, that the Anglo-French entente was not a binding military agreement. However, the kaiser's provocative diplomacy during the crisis had greatly alarmed **Sir Edward Grey**, the British foreign secretary, and he gave firm support to French claims over trade in Morocco at the Algeciras conference.

Morocco's independence was confirmed, but France was given control over the Moroccan central bank, thus giving a significant boost to French economic influence in Morocco. The kaiser's actions had, therefore, served only to heighten fears about German ambitions in France, Britain and Russia, for no real gain.

Anglo-German naval rivalry, 1908–10

The decision of the kaiser to engage in a frantic naval rivalry with Britain was equally counter-productive. The Anglo-German naval race reached fever pitch between 1908 and 1910. The German desire to build a word-class navy was matched by a British, bulldog-style determination to uphold the traditional supremacy of the Royal Navy.

At the heart of the naval race was the production in Germany and Britain of new 'unsinkable' battleships (known as dreadnoughts). The Anglo-German naval race produced pain and tension in both countries, and deeply soured their relations. It was the naval race, Sir Edward Grey claimed, which was the most significant reason why British public opinion turned sharply against Germany, and which encouraged Britain to draw closer to France.

The Bosnian crisis, 1908–09

The Bosnian crisis was another diplomatic affair which served to heighten tension in Europe. In October 1908, Austria-Hungary annexed the Turkish Ottoman province of Bosnia-Herzegovina, located in the Balkans, in response to the growth of 'Young Turk' and Serb nationalism in the region. The tsar expressed Russia's outrage at the annexation, and expected French and British

Sir Edward Grey (1862–1933) was British foreign secretary from 1905 to 1916 (making him the longest-serving holder of the post in the twentieth century). He helped to forge closer ties with France and signed the Anglo-Russian Convention in 1907. He is generally regarded as a shrewd diplomat who placed Britain in a very strong position through diplomacy, thus enabling Britain to play a decisive role in the eventual defeat of Germany in the First World War. He was made a peer, and adopted the title of Grey of Fallodon after the First World War.

support. However, when the kaiser announced that Germany would stand by Austria-Hungary, the French, the Russians and the British all refused to risk a war over the affair. The Bosnian crisis did show the strength of the Triple Alliance, but it made the Russians more determined to increase defence expenditure, in order not to back down in the Balkans again, and also encouraged Russia to draw closer to Serbia.

The Agadir crisis, 1911

In 1911, a second major diplomatic crisis erupted in Morocco which brought Europe near to war. In May 1911, French troops helped the sultan of Morocco to stop a nationalist revolt in Fez. The German government saw the arrival of French troops in Morocco as a pretext for French annexation of the territory. In July 1911, a German gunboat (*The Panther*) arrived in Agadir, with the aim of gaining some trading concessions from the French. The French government, supported by Sir Edward Grey, offered none. The German government was forced to withdraw *The Panther* from Agadir. In October 1911, the German government agreed to recognise French dominance over Agadir, and received only a small amount of French territory in the Congo in return.

The Agadir crisis was one of the most crucial events in the years which led to the outbreak of war, for a number of reasons. It drew Britain and France into much closer co-operation against the German threat. It showed that France (unlike in the previous Moroccan crisis in 1905) could no longer be bullied by Germany. More importantly, Germany was now in a very weakened diplomatic position. In any future European crisis, it was unlikely any power would suffer the humiliation of backing down.

The Balkan Wars, 1912–13

Between 1912 and 1914, the focus of European tension switched away from great-power conflict in Africa towards ethnic rivalry among nationalist groups in the Balkans. There were a number of rival powers in the Balkans, most notably Bulgaria, Albania and Macedonia, all united in a determination to break free from the ailing Turkish Ottoman Empire. A number of other Balkan powers, including Serbia, Romania, Greece and Montenegro, also desired to make territorial gains in the region when Ottoman rule collapsed.

By 1912, Serbia, by means of skilful diplomacy, managed to create the Balkan League (which also included Greece, Bulgaria and Montenegro). The central aim of the Balkan League was to destroy the power of the Ottoman Empire in the region. In October 1912, the Balkan League attacked Turkey, beginning the First Balkan War, and gained a stunning victory, which drove the Ottoman rulers out of the Balkans. The diplomatic agreement which followed the First Balkan War (the London Agreement of 1913) divided up the

European territory of the Ottoman Empire, except Albania, between Serbia, Bulgaria and Greece. But the Serbian government was outraged at not gaining an Adriatic port, and the Greeks and the Bulgarians also felt dissatisfied with their territorial gains.

The volatile Balkan League soon fell apart. In June 1913, Bulgaria attacked Serbia, starting the Second Balkan War. However, Greece, Romania and Turkey all declared war on Bulgaria. The Bulgarian army was quickly defeated. Under the Treaty of Bucharest (1913) the Bulgarians were forced to give Serbia large parts of Macedonia.

The consequences of the Balkan Wars were far reaching. The Ottoman rulers had been driven out of the Balkans, but this did not bring stability to the region. Serbian power had been greatly increased. Indeed, the growing power of Serbia in the Balkans was viewed with growing concern by Austria-Hungary, primarily because Serbian nationalists were determined to support other nationalist groups that wanted to break free of Austro-Hungarian rule, particularly in Bosnia-Herzegovina. The Austro-Hungarian government was, therefore, determined not to allow Serbia to profit ever again from the instability in the Balkans. With Serbia in close alliance with Russia, and Austria-Hungary allied with Germany, there remained a real prospect that a future Balkan conflict could quite easily escalate into a European war.

> Draw up a list in order of significance of the major events in the period 1908–11 that affected international relations.

Which nation was most to blame for the outbreak of the First World War?

The war plans of the great powers

One of the major consequences of the growth of tension in Europe in the years from 1900 to 1914 was that it encouraged the military planners of the major powers to draw up plans for a possible war. Germany, Austria-Hungary, France and Russia all made plans for a swift mobilisation of troops at the outbreak of any major conflict in Europe. The British government had also made plans to send an expeditionary force to France in the event of a German attack. The politicians and rulers of Europe faced pressure from these military planners, who believed it was vital to seize the military initiative at the outset of military hostilities. The most detailed of these military plans was the Schlieffen plan, drawn up by a German general in 1905. This plan was designed to launch a German military attack against France through Belgium to achieve a swift victory, and then to turn the bulk of the German forces towards the defeat of Russia. It was the swift implementation of this plan which brought France and Britain into the First World War. Even so, it must be remembered that the politicians and rulers of the major powers had the final say – not the military planners.

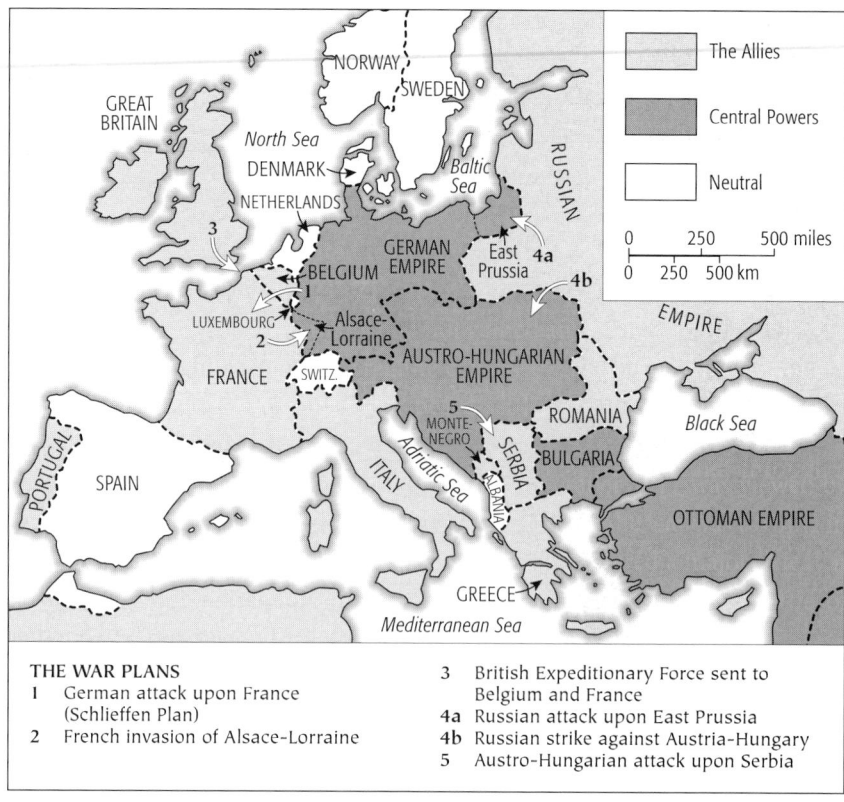

THE WAR PLANS

1 German attack upon France
(Schlieffen Plan)
2 French invasion of Alsace-Lorraine

3 British Expeditionary Force sent to
Belgium and France
4a Russian attack upon East Prussia
4b Russian strike against Austria-Hungary
5 Austro-Hungarian attack upon Serbia

Map 1. The war plans of the European powers.

The July crisis, 1914

The final crisis in Europe which led to the outbreak of the First World War came again in the volatile Balkan region. Once more, Austria-Hungary and Germany were deeply involved. The starting point of what became dubbed the 'July crisis' was the assassination of Archduke Franz Ferdinand, the nephew of Franz Josef I, the Austrian emperor, which actually took place in Sarajevo on 28 June 1914. The assassin was Gavrilo Princip, a Bosnian terrorist, with close links to the Black Hand, a Serbian terrorist organisation. The Serbian government had no direct link to the assassination, but this was not believed by the Austrian government, which decided to use the incident to settle accounts with Serbia.

On 4 July 1914, Franz Josef I asked Kaiser Wilhelm II for German support to eliminate Serbian power in the Balkans. The next day, the kaiser gave his unqualified support (known as 'the blank cheque') to Austria-Hungary for an attack on Serbia, although he hoped such a war could remain localised.

The crisis mounted throughout the final days of a very sunny July. On 23 July 1914, Austria sent an **ultimatum** to Serbia, which demanded that the Serbs must allow the Austrian police to enter Serbia with the aim of

An **ultimatum** is a final warning used in diplomatic relations as a threat to a rival nation to agree to some conditions or face economic penalties or war.

Archduke Franz Ferdinand arriving at Sarajevo. Later that day he and his pregnant wife Sophie were assassinated.

arresting all anti-Habsburg terrorist groups. The Serbian government would not agree to this demand, but did offer to take part in an international conference to settle outstanding differences with Austria-Hungary. On 28 July 1914, Austria-Hungary declared war on Serbia, in the hope that Russia, Serbia's ally, would not intervene. However, the tsar made clear his determination to defend Serbia. The German government responded by informing the tsar that if Russia went to the defence of Serbia, the German army would go to the defence of Austria-Hungary. To make matters worse, the French pledged to stand by Russia in the event of a German attack. In this way, a minor quarrel between Austria and Serbia was escalating into a major European crisis.

The German government made no attempt to restrain Austria-Hungary throughout the July crisis. Indeed, the kaiser escalated the crisis by sending the Russian government an ultimatum, on 31 July 1914, which said that unless Russia ceased mobilising its troops in support of Serbia, then Germany would declare war on Russia. The tsar refused to stop Russian mobilisation and, on 1 August, Germany did declare war on Russia.

The following day, Germany sent a blunt ultimatum to Belgium asking for permission for the safe passage of its troops through its territory, for what now seemed an inevitable attack on France (on the pretext that France was Russia's military ally). On 3 August 1914, Germany invaded Belgium and also declared war on France.

On 4 August 1914, the British government declared war on Germany on the grounds of Germany's breach of Belgian neutrality. But Sir Edward Grey had long realised that Britain had to support France and Russia in order to prevent Germany dominating Europe by force.

Identify three major reasons why the July crisis escalated into war.

As the July crisis escalated, opposition to the war in most European capitals evaporated. When war was declared there was actually cheering in the streets of Germany, Britain, France, Russia, Austria-Hungary and Serbia. For many years before the outbreak of the First World War, war had seemed inevitable to most Europeans. When it arrived, it came as a relief from years of mounting tension. No power was willing to back down in July 1914. Yet it was the German government, by its actions, which had escalated a minor quarrel between Austria-Hungary and Serbia into a major European war, which developed into a world war.

What caused the war?

Five key factors played a part in causing the First World War:

1 the dispute between Austria-Hungary and Serbia;
2 the role played by Russia in the July crisis;
3 the role played by Germany in the July crisis;
4 the alliance system;
5 the war plans of the major powers.

The most dominant short-term cause of the war was the dispute between Austria-Hungary and Serbia. This dispute became explosive following the assassination of Franz Ferdinand, which provided the perfect opportunity for Austria-Hungary to gain public support for a war against the ambitious Serbs. However, while Habsburg–Serb antagonism explains why these two countries went to war, it does not explain why this conflict escalated into a full-scale European conflict. Quite clearly, other factors have to be taken into account.

The role played by Russia in the July crisis requires consideration. The Russian decision to stand by Serbia probably made Serbia less willing to agree to Austro-Hungarian demands than might otherwise have been the case. The tsar's decision to mobilise his troops against Austria-Hungary was another contributory factor in escalating the crisis, because it gave the German government a perfect opportunity to enter the crisis as the defender of its alliance partner. It must be emphasised, however, that Russia had every right to defend its ally from attack, and the tsar did attempt to bring about a negotiated settlement of the crisis, which was rejected by Austria-Hungary and Germany. It is probably worth adding that Russia's determination not to back down against German aggression was largely due to widely held fears that Germany intended to gain territory in Europe at Russia's expense, fears which Germany's high-handed actions during the July crisis tended to confirm.

The role of Germany during the July crisis is more significant than the actions of Austria-Hungary, Serbia or Russia. The German government, far from attempting to restrain Austria-Hungary, openly encouraged the Habsburg monarchy to attack Serbia, and made no attempt to seek a peaceful conclusion to the crisis. These actions appear to give credence to the view that Germany used the minor Habsburg–Serb quarrel as a pretext to launch its own bid to escape from **diplomatic encirclement** by launching a European war.

The importance of the alliance system must also be considered in explaining the outbreak of war. Germany was determined to support its Triple Alliance partner during the crisis, but followed its own aims. The Russians were determined to support Serbia, and the French were determined to support Russia, but each power decided to go to war not because of alliance commitments, but by deciding what was best for its own national interest. It must be remembered that Britain had no firm alliance with France or Russia, but went to war all the same, which indicates that national interests, not diplomatic agreements, were once again pre-eminent.

The role played by the war plans of the major powers in accelerating the crisis into war must also be evaluated. All the European powers had developed detailed military plans in the expectation of war. The generals had advised the politicians that the swift mobilisation of forces was required in the event of war. These views certainly increased the tempo of events. However, British plans for mobilisation were very poor, and the French army had no offensive strategy. In Russia, the tsar – not the generals – took the vital decision to mobilise the troops. Only in Germany, and to a lesser extent Austria-Hungary, did existing war plans play a vital role. The German generals certainly put pressure on the kaiser to implement the Schlieffen plan, which made sure this crisis would end in the outbreak of a major European war. Nevertheless, the views of the German generals were in harmony with those of the kaiser and, in any case, it was only in Germany that the military planners had the most decisive influence over events.

The role of economic factors

The concentration on the political, military and diplomatic causes of war has tended to relegate economic issues to the background. At one time, only left-wing historians (usually supporters of the economic theories of Karl Marx)

Diplomatic encirclement is a position in which a power or group of powers faces a stronger group of allies.

Give a brief
explanation of which
was the most
significant factor in
bringing about the
outbreak of the First
World War.

argued that the foreign policy decisions of the major powers were determined
by underlying economic desires to win wars in order to advance the outlets for
business, trade and investment. The problem with this view is finding how
business influenced the politicians in their decisions for war. The capitalists in
Britain and France certainly did not want war, and even in Germany the key
industrialists did not believe they needed war to increase profits. It seems the
actual decision makers in government went to war without any full appreci-
ation of the possible economic consequences.

Historical interpretation: the origins of the war

There has been a lively debate over the origins of the First World War. It
began almost as soon as the killing on the battlefield finally stopped. At the
Paris peace conference, the major blame for starting the war was placed by
the peacemakers (who had won the war) on Germany and its chief ally
Austria-Hungary (which had lost). However, the verdict of the winners did
not endure for very long. During the inter-war years, historians started to
claim the war was a tragedy of miscalculation by all the major powers, and
that they all should share some of the blame. It came to be accepted during
the inter-war years that there was no general will to start a major European
war in 1914, and that a small crisis in the Balkans quickly escalated, producing a world war which no single country had truly wanted.

   This 'shared guilt' interpretation of the outbreak of the First World War
was challenged only in the early 1960s, by Fritz Fischer, a German historian, who claimed that the German government realised, and hoped, that by
egging on Austria-Hungary in its quarrel with Serbia it could launch a
European war, which would gain for Germany a dominant position in
Europe. Fischer also showed there was a strong will to launch a war by
German leaders in 1914, and that the peacemakers were right: the German
government was principally responsible for the outbreak of the First World
War. Although many historians originally challenged Fischer's views, by
the mid-1980s Norman Stone conceded that 'not many historians now-
adays dissent from the proposition that the German government . . . delib-
erately provoked the war of 1914'. Much recent research has also indicated
that Russia, Britain and France all wanted to avoid military conflict in
1914, and intervened to prevent the German domination of Europe. As a
result of this new research, issues such as the war plans of the great powers,
the role of the alliance system and the Austro–Serb quarrel are now seen as
contributory factors in producing the growing tension in Europe before
1914, but not as the central reasons why war broke out. Indeed, within the
current historical debate, the original view, advanced by the peacemakers

at the Paris conference, that Germany and Austria-Hungary started the First World War, and dragged the rest of Europe into the conflict, is widely accepted as the most logical explanation, supported by the evidence of the sources.

Summary questions

1 Identify and explain *two* reasons for the growth of tension in Europe in the period 1890–1914.

2 Compare the importance of at least *three* factors which led to the outbreak of war in 1914.

3 The First World War and its consequences

- ◆ Why was there a stalemate on the western front for most of the First World War?
- ◆ What were the social and economic effects of the First World War on the civilian populations of Britain and Germany?
- ◆ Why did Germany lose the war?
- ◆ What were the consequences of the war?

Significant dates

1914   *August*   Germany invades Belgium and then north-eastern France on the western front, and attacks Russia on the eastern front
     October–November   First Battle of Ypres
     November   Ottoman Empire joins the war on side of Central powers

1915   *April*   Poison gas first used (by German army) at Second Battle of Ypres
     25 April   Allied troops land at Gallipoli (and are eventually forced to evacuate in January 1916)
     May   Italy declares war on Austria-Hungary

1916   *May*   Battle of Jutland (only major naval battle of the war)
     July–November   Battle of the Somme, which sees the first use, by Britain, of the tank
     December   Lloyd George becomes British prime minister

1917   *April*   USA enters the war on the side of the Allies

1918   *January*   Woodrow Wilson, US president, publishes his '14 points', which lay the basis of the subsequent peace settlement
     March   Russia signs the punitive Treaty of Brest-Litovsk with Germany
     March   Germany's final offensive begins on the western front
     July–November   Allied counter-offensive on the western front finally breaks through the German defences
     October   Mutiny of German sailors at Kiel
     30 October   Ottoman Empire concludes armistice with Allies
     3 November   Austria-Hungary concludes armistice with Allies
     9 November   Kaiser Wilhelm II abdicates
     11 November   Victory for the Allies is confirmed by the signing of the armistice between them and Germany

Overview

Most generals expected the First World War to last only a matter of weeks. Yet this bloody conflict lasted four and a half years and claimed over 8.5 million dead, and 22 million wounded and disabled. Over 4 million women lost their husbands in the conflict, and 8 million children lost fathers. The total cost of the war has been put at the staggering sum of £260 billion.

The First World War began in July 1914, in a mood of popular excitement, with old-fashioned cavalry charges, more suited to nineteenth-century warfare. It ended in November 1918 with modern weapons such as tanks, aircraft and heavy artillery weapons. The two rival power groupings at the beginning of the war were the Triple Entente – the 'Allies' (Britain, France and Russia) – and the Central powers (Germany and Austria-Hungary).

Why was there a stalemate on the western front for most of the First World War?

The western front

The German army expected to win the war by launching a devastating attack on France, followed by an equally decisive attack on Russia in eastern Europe. This was the Schlieffen plan (see Chapter 2), and it very nearly came off. The French army, supported by the British Expeditionary Force (BEF), were initially surprised by the strength of the German assault, which moved remorselessly through Belgium, and advanced on to French territory. The German assault on France was halted by the BEF at Mons in August 1914, and even more decisively by the French army at the Battle of the Marne in September 1914, when the German army was forced to retreat to the River Aisne.

It is often assumed that the German army was technically and tactically superior, and made a mistake by choosing to fight a defensive war on the western front after making initial territorial gains. The German high command were certainly better trained in the art of war than any of their opponents, but they rejected the use of lorries for transport and made much greater use of horses. In 1914, the German commander, General Alexander von Kluck, used 84,000 horses. Indeed, the food needs of the horses greatly increased the supply problems of the German army.

By the end of September 1914, the Schlieffen plan had failed. Germany now faced a war on two fronts, in western and eastern Europe. Soldiers on both sides on the western front set about digging a line of trenches, separated by a barbed wire 'no-man's-land', which ultimately stretched from the Swiss border to the English Channel. The German army built an almost impregnable triple line of trenches. They had a much better communication system between the high command and the soldiers in the trenches than the British and French. The Germans also developed better steel helmets, flame-throwers and hand grenades. In addition, the Germans made better use of barbed wire. All these technical advantages of the German army help to explain the very high level of casualties among those British and French armies which attempted to mount offensives against the German positions during the war. The massed trenches on both sides ensured there was a stale-mate, with very little mobility on the western front in the first three years of the war.

The German army remained on the defensive during most of 1915. It was in 1916 that the First World War started to assume a very bloody character, with both sides making bold – and ultimately futile – attempts to break the deadlock, most notably at the Battle of Verdun (which lasted for most of that year), which saw a combined death toll on both sides of 700,000, and at the Battle of the Somme (from July to November). The latter resulted in the British army losing 60,000 on the first day, and by the end Britain had lost 418,000 troops; German deaths numbered 450,000 and French losses were 194,000 at the Somme. Verdun and the Somme were the two most bloody battles on the western front during the First World War. A close third in terms of casualties was the Third Battle of Ypres, in 1917.

In all these deadly battles, mass infantry attacks were beaten back by the use of heavy artillery, with little territorial gains for either side. The defending armies were able to take advantage of important technical developments in fire power provided by the large artillery gun, the magazine rifle and the machine gun, which became the most potent weapon on the battleground, and rendered the cavalry charge, which had dominated many battles in the nineteenth century, virtually useless.

The generals on both sides were blamed (by contemporary soldiers and subsequent historians) for their heartless lack of concern for human life on the western front, which contributed to the high death toll. It was said of the leading British general (Douglas Haig) that he killed more English soldiers than the German army.

Haig's diaries do reveal a startling indifference to the mounting number of deaths on the western front. More recently, the exceptionally difficult task faced by the generals has been highlighted by some 'revisionist' historians, who have claimed the generals were trying to turn largely untrained soldiers into an efficient modern army in a short space of time. It is probably worth adding that the generals were also under great pressure, from their govern-ments, and from public opinion at home, to gain a decisive victory and win the war.

A **revisionist historian** is one who attempts to revise an orthodox or accepted view of events. A very extreme revisionist might suggest that Hitler was not responsible for the Holocaust.

Identify three reasons why a stalemate developed on the western front.

German dead in the devastated landscape created by the Battle of the Somme, October 1916.

What were the social and economic effects of the First World War on the civilian populations of Britain and Germany?

The very high death toll in the war strained the human and economic resources of all the major powers to the limit. The events on the battlefield were directly felt by families on the 'home front'. As the war dragged on, a very high premium was placed on the economic and organisational abilities of each national government involved in the conflict. The arms expenditure of the rival powers rose from 4 per cent of national income in 1914 to a staggering 25 per cent by the end of 1916. A great many factories in Britain, France, Germany and Russia were turned over completely to munitions production.

To pay for the war, Britain and France raised taxes and borrowed money – especially from the USA. The German government pushed up its national debt to quite staggering proportions in the hope that victory in war would enable it to pay it off. However, the greatest economic and military strain was felt by those nations which lacked modern industry, most notably Russia, Austria-Hungary and Italy. The modern industrial economies of Europe – Germany, Britain and France – rose to the challenge of war much better than the old pre-industrial societies.

Germany

The German government created a system in which leading army figures and top industrialists co-operated in running the wartime economy. State corporations were set up to organise the provision of vital commodities and raw materials necessary to supply the needs of the armed forces. In October 1916, the 'Hindenburg programme' intensified state and army control of the German economy. Machinery was transferred from industries dependent on the domestic market to munitions factories. Many companies which did not contribute to the war effort were forced by the state to close. The effect of this ruthless organisation of industry by the German state was to create great industrial monopoly companies and cartels which controlled the provision of raw materials, and it led to shortages and deprivation for ordinary citizens on the home front. The needs of the German armed forces came ahead of those of the civilian population. The German army high command was able to place pressure on the kaiser to limit the powers of parliament and to sanction a national service law to allow the unrestricted **conscription** of citizens to aid the war effort in military or industrial service. Indeed, Germany during the war was a virtual army–big-business dictatorship, which put all its effort into achieving the goal of victory in the war and suspended all the constitutional liberties enjoyed by the citizen in peacetime. Walter Rathenau, a leading German industrialist, called the organisation of the German war effort 'state socialism', implying that every individual was equally serving the needs and aims of the state. This idea was something which was later adopted more fully during the era of the Third Reich.

Britain

The British government moved more slowly towards greater state control of the war effort. Indeed, one of the most popular slogans used by the Liberal government in 1914 was 'Business as Usual'. It was only in 1916, for example, that conscription was introduced in Britain, whereas most other countries in Europe had schemes of conscription before 1914. The idea of forcing a person to serve in the army went against the Liberal ideal of free will. Hence, the British army was based on the 'voluntary principle', whereby a recruit chose to join. After the appointment of **David Lloyd George** as prime minister in December 1916, however, the labour force and the economy were more centrally organised and state interference in the economy became normal.

Women began to take over work previously done only by men in key war industries such as munitions, engineering and transport. The employment of women in Britain increased from 3.5 million to 5 million from 1914 to 1918. The war effort had given women the opportunity to show they could compete in what had previously been described as 'a man's world'. As a result, the status

Conscription relates to compulsory service in the armed forces by all able-bodied males within a particular age range. In Germany conscription was also used to call up people to serve in industry.

David Lloyd George (1863–1945) was the British prime minister from 1916 until 1922. As chancellor of the exchequer from 1908 to 1915 he was instrumental in introducing ambitious schemes of social reform. He played a leading role at the Paris peace conference, where he attempted – without success – to prevent Germany being treated harshly. He always feared the Treaty of Versailles might provoke Germans to embark on a 'war of revenge'. He resigned as prime minister in 1922. He spent the rest of his political career as a colourful and controversial public figure, mistrusted by the Liberals, who never forgave him for splitting the party during the war. His public image was further damaged by accusations (which turned out to be true) that he sold honours for cash and carried on a string of extra-marital affairs. He was made a peer in his later years, adopting the title of 1st Earl of Dwyfor.

Women and men working in a munitions factory.

of women was greatly enhanced during the war. In 1918, women were granted the vote in British national elections for the first time.

The co-operation of trade unions with the government facilitated the introduction of longer working hours, which speeded up production in industry. This helped to increase the status of trade unions in the years which followed the war, and aided the growth of support for the Labour Party. The British government also increased its control over the presentation of the war in the press by appointing a minister of propaganda. To pay for the war, indirect taxes were greatly increased in Britain on goods.

> Identify two groups whose role was enhanced during the First World War.

Why did Germany lose the war?

Attempts to break the deadlock

Each side in the conflict looked for a new way to achieve a decisive breakthrough. The Allies used a naval blockade in an attempt to starve the Central powers of vital supplies of food and raw materials. The torpedo and the mine were used extensively in naval battles. The guns on British battleships were 15 inches wide and could be used with devastating effect against enemy vessels. Another new, state-of-the-art naval vessel – the torpedo-destroyer – was also used to deadly effect by the Royal Navy during the conflict. These technical advances helped the British to enjoy command of the seas and put into effect the naval blockade. However, the blockade worked only very slowly.

The Germans responded with a naval blockade of Russia (helped by Turkey), and engaged in 'unrestricted' submarine warfare directed against the trade of Britain, France and Italy, which meant that Germany would attack vessels even of non-combatant powers (such as the USA) if they entered the war zone. However, unrestricted submarine warfare ultimately proved counter-productive because it inflamed neutral powers, particularly the USA.

The most significant naval battle of the war (the Battle of Jutland, 1916) produced no clear outcome, even though the Germans could claim victory as their navy sank 14 ships compared with 11 sunk by the British. A more important consequence of the Battle of Jutland was that it convinced the German navy it had to avoid further naval battles. After Jutland, the German navy returned to port, leaving Britain with control of the seas, at least on the surface of the water.

Another attempt to break the deadlock was to open up a new front. Winston Churchill, the first lord of the admiralty, made a proposal to land British Empire forces by sea at the Gallipoli peninsula, at the western entrance to the Dardanelles. The aim of the Gallipoli campaign was to open up a new front in south-east Europe by defeating Turkey, a leading German ally, and hopefully bring Bulgaria over to the Allied side. The Gallipoli plan led to failure and embarrassment for the British government. Churchill was so damaged by the fiasco he was forced to resign. The British troops, supported by Australian and New Zealand forces, did manage a landing by sea at Gallipoli in April 1915, but they never got much beyond the beach and were effectively beaten back and comprehensively defeated by the defending Turkish forces, whose abilities in warfare had been seriously underestimated. Even worse, Bulgaria signed an alliance with Germany and Turkey in the aftermath of the Gallipoli fiasco and thereby increased the pressure on Russia on the eastern front.

New weapons were also tried out with the aim of achieving a breakthrough on the western front, including poison gas, airships, tanks and aircraft. The British were the first to introduce the tank into warfare, but early models were very slow and kept breaking down. It was only towards the end of the war that these teething problems were solved, and tanks did make a significant contribution to the advance of the Allies in the final offensive against Germany on the western front in the summer of 1918. There was a greater use of motorised transport as the war progressed. In 1914, the British army had 1,000 lorries, but by 1918 this figure had shot up to 60,000. The potential of aircraft was not

A tank crossing British trenches in 1917.

fully understood at the outbreak of the war. The first aeroplanes used in combat in 1914 were small and travelled at low speeds. In fact, airships, which were used for reconnaissance, proved more reliable than aeroplanes during the early stages of the war and were used more extensively. As the war developed, the original teething problems of the early aeroplanes started to be overcome: their range increased; they could travel faster; and their bombing potential started to be exploited. By the end of the war, the aeroplane had started to become an indispensable weapon in modern warfare.

Identify and explain three attempts to break the deadlock.

The search for allies

A search for new allies was another method used by both sides to break the deadlock. The Allies attracted more powerful nations: Japan joined the war in August 1914, seizing German colonies in China and the Pacific. Italy had opted for neutrality at the outset of the conflict, but after protracted diplomatic negotiations with the Allies, and the promise of territorial gains in the event of victory, decided to join their side in 1915. Romania (1916) and Greece (1917) also joined the struggle on the side of the Allies. In contrast, the new allies who joined the war on the side of the Central powers tended to be small, militarily weak powers, notably Turkey (1914) and Bulgaria (1915).

The most significant new entrant to the First World War was unquestionably the USA, which entered the war in April 1917 as an 'associate' of the

This powerful poster attracted tens of thousands of young American men to fight in their country's armed services.

Assess which side gained most from the search for allies.

Allies, primarily because Germany refused to end unrestricted submarine attacks against US shipping. Yet even the entry of the USA, with its massive economic muscle, made no immediate military impact. In 1917, the US army numbered only 130,000 men. By the beginning of 1918, however, US finance, military supplies and the vast expansion of the US army started to make an important contribution to wearing Germany down on the western front. For instance, the US army sent 2 million troops to Europe in 1918.

War aims

The entry of the USA was also important in another respect: it helped the Allies to define more clearly what they were fighting for. Woodrow Wilson, the US president, gave fresh impetus to the Allied cause by claiming they were fighting the war to achieve two clear aims:

1 to uphold democratic principles;
2 to defend the right of small nations to govern themselves (national self-determination).

On 8 January 1918, Wilson laid down his '14 points' in a major speech. This was the clearest statement of Allied war aims. Among Wilson's recommendations were demands for a future 'new world order', to be based on open diplomacy, freedom of trade, disarmament and the rights of small states to govern themselves. A League of Nations, which would provide a safeguard against the possibility of a future war, was also promised by Wilson as part of the peace settlement at the end of the conflict.

The war aims of Woodrow Wilson seem idealistic when compared with those of Germany. The 'September Programme', a key statement of German war aims, drawn up by **Theobald von Bethmann-Hollweg**, the German chancellor, in 1914, outlined four expansionist objectives:

1 to weaken France to such an extent as to make its revival as a great power 'impossible for all time';
2 to break Russian dominance in eastern Europe by bringing all non-Russian areas under German domination;
3 to achieve German economic dominance in Europe (*Mitteleuropa*) through the creation of a vast common market;
4 to establish a large central-African German empire.

The eastern front

The war on the eastern front was more mobile than the war in the west of Europe. It was believed that the vast human resources of Russia, dubbed the 'Russian steamroller', would enable the Russians to bleed the German army to death on the eastern front, provided they received adequate supplies of food and military equipment. But the Russian generals had fewer troops available than did the German and Austro-Hungarian generals at the start of the war.

In September 1914, the Russian army was twice defeated by the German army, at the Battles of Tannenberg and the Masurian Lakes. In these early battlefield exchanges, the Russian army lost a great many troops and much vital equipment. It performed much better against the weaker Austro-Hungarian army in Serbia, gaining a very important victory at Galicia in September 1914, when over 100,000 prisoners were taken. The weakness of the Austro-Hungarian army proved a severe liability to the Germans on the eastern front as they were often forced to bail them out of tricky situations.

During 1915, the Russians suffered further defeats as the German army mounted a successful offensive in eastern Europe, capturing most of Poland along the way. In June 1916, the Russian army, commanded by General Brusilov, launched a successful offensive in the east, which brought the Austro-Hungarian army to the verge of collapse. But the Brusilov offensive was the last great effort by the Russian army. For the remainder of 1916 a stalemate developed on the eastern front.

Evaluate the war aims of Germany.

Theobald von Bethmann-Hollweg (1856–1921) was German chancellor from 1909 to 1917. He was a skilled administrator, but lacked diplomatic skills. As a result, Germany became increasingly isolated diplomatically in the years before the First World War. During the July crisis, he famously offered Austria-Hungary a 'blank cheque' to deal with Serbia. He adopted a strong nationalist stand during the war and outlined aims for vast German territorial expansion in eastern Europe. He fell from power in 1917 as his handling of the war came under increasing criticism in the German parliament. He died a largely discredited figure.

In July 1917, a major Russian offensive failed to achieve a breakthrough. Mutiny now spread throughout the ranks of the Russian army. In October 1917, when the Bolshevik Party seized power, the new government, led by Lenin, opened peace negotiations with the Central powers at Brest-Litovsk. The terms imposed by Germany on Russia under the Treaty of Brest-Litovsk (1918) were extremely harsh. The Bolshevik government conceded 33 per cent of its territory, which accounted for 64 per cent of its pig iron production, 40 per cent of coal output and 24 per cent of steel-making capacity.

On the eastern front, Germany had not gained an outright military victory, but had won because the tsarist regime collapsed, and the new revolutionary government decided to conclude a peace settlement with Germany rather than continue with the war.

The withdrawal of Russia from the war in November 1917 was viewed by the Allies as a body blow. At the close of 1917, it seemed the war was turning in Germany's favour, especially as the Italians had also suffered a major defeat at the hands of the German and Austrian combined forces at the Battle of Caporetto in October 1917.

The defeat of Germany on the western front

However, the strain of war, and the 'silent dictatorship' of the army, was producing large-scale economic problems and political unrest in Germany throughout 1917 and 1918. Food was in very short supply, strikes had become commonplace in key industries and the revolutionary Social Democratic Party was agitating for an end to the war. In July 1917, many deputies in the Reichstag called for a negotiated peace. Bethmann-Hollweg became the scapegoat for all this internal unrest, and was forced to resign. In January 1918, a wave of strikes broke out in Berlin, and demonstrators demanded an end to the bitter conflict on the western front.

The German army, ignoring this growing opposition to the war, went ahead with plans for its largest offensive of the war. In March 1918, Germany launched a final make-or-break offensive on the western front (the Ludendorff offensive). This final gamble by the Germans to win the war, before their supplies ran out, came very close to success. They broke through at the River Somme, and were less than 40 miles from Paris by the end of May 1918. At the end of July 1918, however, the German attack was finally halted by the Allies. In August, the Allies, under the overall command of Marshal Foch, the French commander, began what proved to be the most decisive counter-attack of the entire war on the western front. This dare-devil assault finally punched a large hole through German defences, sending the German army into retreat. In September 1918, the Austro-Hungarian government appealed for peace, followed by the Bulgarians.

The leading German generals (Erich Ludendorff and Paul von Hindenburg) now realised the war was lost. They advised leading figures in the Reichstag to form a democratic government in order to negotiate peace terms, before the Allies occupied German territory. This decision, taken by the leaders of the German army, was designed to shift the blame for defeat onto the shoulders of the democratic politicians, and away from the kaiser and the army – the real architects of Germany's defeat. It helped to feed a powerful myth, which held that the German army was not defeated in battle, but 'stabbed in the back' by socialists and democrats at home. The kaiser abdicated and fled into exile in Holland. A new German democratic government was formed. At 5 a.m. on 11 November 1918, the armistice was signed with the Allies, and at exactly 11 a.m. the First World War ended.

The reasons for the German defeat

The German army came very close to winning the First World War, but in the end was defeated by a more powerful combination of allies. The failure of the Schlieffen plan ensured the Germans had to fight a protracted war on two fronts, which sapped Germany's economic and military resources. At sea, the Allied blockade proved crucial, because Germany started to suffer serious shortages of food and raw materials, especially during 1918. The entry of the USA into the war, which was actually caused by the German policy of unrestricted submarine warfare, brought a very powerful ally to the side of Britain and France, at a time when the Allies were under pressure. This ensured that, in the long term, Germany could not hope to win. The German army also suffered from having very weak allies, which it constantly had to help out of trouble. This overstretched the Germans' economic and military resources even further.

In the final analysis, the economic and military strength of the Allies proved stronger than that of Germany over the course of a lengthy conflict. In this respect, the decision of the British government to go to war in 1914 was a decisive factor which tipped the scales against Germany. The British put over 7 million troops into the battles on the western front. This enabled the French to hold out against the German army on land, something they had not achieved in the Franco-Prussian War of 1870–71, and failed to achieve in 1940. Of course, British and French losses were enormous but, in the course of battle, the Germans lost many of their best troops as the conflict developed. As a result, the superior military strength of Germany was gradually worn down. By 1918, the entry of the Americans, which added a further 2 million troops, and even more economic muscle than Britain and France, ensured that the balance of forces ranged against Germany was much too strong for one single nation, supported only by weak military allies, to resist.

Draw up a list in order of significance of the reasons why Germany lost the war.

What were the consequences of the war?

The First World War had far-reaching consequences. During the four years of conflict, four major monarchical empires (Hohenzollern – Germany; Romanov – Russia; Habsburg – Austria-Hungary; and Ottoman – Turkey) were destroyed. The cost of the war in loss of life was enormous. There were over 8.5 million killed in combat and 22 million wounded or disabled. Most of the casualties were young, able-bodied men (dubbed the 'lost generation'). There were a great many widows and orphans after the war.

The economic consequences of the war were also far reaching. The world economy suffered a slump after the war, which damaged world currencies, trade and employment. The switching of production to war materials led to unemployment after the war, and increases in the price of consumer goods. Another major economic consequence was a vast increase in the debts of most nations. Most of these debts were owed to the USA. As a result, the war severely weakened the economic dominance of Europe, and saw the growth of the economic power of the USA.

The war also produced many other changes. There was a great increase in state power in most European countries. The Russian Revolution of 1917 began the trend towards totalitarian governments, which became a feature of the inter-war period. The war also led to demands by small nations to govern themselves. Attitudes towards war were also affected by the conflict. There was a new drive towards pacifism, illustrated by the rapid growth of peace movements and anti-war literature and art during the inter-war period. These feelings were not shared by some ex-soldiers, especially in Germany and Italy, who looked back with pride at the comradeship of the trenches, and formed national movements which aimed to restore military strength.

In addition, the war also saw a change in the status of women. Many had been employed in munitions factories and in transport and clerical work during the war, and many demanded greater equality in the inter-war period. This increased status was recognised by women getting the vote in elections for the first time. Finally, the war also increased the power and status of organised labour, and there was a growth of trade union representation after the war.

The First World War was a great accelerator of events in Europe. It left the politicians of the nations which had won it with the daunting task of devising a peace settlement which ensured that such a war would not break out again.

Identify three major consequences of the First World War.

Summary questions

1 Compare the importance of at least *three* factors which affected the lives of the civilian population during the First World War.

2 Identify and explain any *two* means used to try to break the deadlock on the western front from 1914 to 1918.

4 The Paris peace settlement and its aftermath, 1919–33

Focus questions

◆ What were the major difficulties facing the peacemakers in 1919?

◆ What were the aims of the peacemakers?

◆ How fair was the Treaty of Versailles towards Germany?

◆ How successful was the League of Nations in encouraging international co-operation from 1920 to 1933?

Significant dates

1918   *November* Armistice is signed between the victorious Allies and the defeated Central powers
December Lloyd George wins the British general election promising electors to 'make Germany pay' the cost of the First World War

1919   *January* Paris peace conference opens at the Palace of Versailles
June Treaty of Versailles is signed 'under protest' by the German government
September Treaty of St Germain is signed by representatives from the Austrian delegation

1920   *January* League of Nations is established
March US senate refuses to ratify Treaty of Versailles and US government signs separate peace treaty with Germany
June Treaty of Trianon is signed by Hungary
August Treaty of Sèvres is signed by Turkey

1921   Allies set Germany's reparations at 132 million marks (£6,600 million at 1921 prices)

1922   Washington naval conference establishes limits on the building of warships by Britain, the USA, Japan, France and Italy

1923   *January* French and Belgian troops occupy the Ruhr industrial region of Germany in an attempt to force the German government to pay reparations (they withdraw at the end of 1923)
July Treaty of Lausanne brings final peace settlement between the Allies and Turkey

1924   *August* Dawes plan reduces German reparation payments and the US government grants the German government a loan to meet payments and to stabilise the German currency, which collapsed in the 'great inflation' that gripped Germany throughout 1923

1925	*October* Locarno Treaties, which accept the western frontiers laid down by Versailles, are signed by Germany
1926	Germany joins the League of Nations
1931	Japan invades Manchuria, but the League of Nations fails to remove Japanese troops
1932	World disarmament conference opens, but does not gain agreement from the major powers for arms limitations
1933	Germany leaves the League of Nations and a new era of tension in Europe begins

Overview

It was in January 1919, at the sumptuous Palace of Versailles, that the first session of the famous Paris peace conference began. The leaders of 32 nations were present to discuss the terms to be imposed on the defeated Central powers (Germany, Austria-Hungary, Bulgaria and Turkey) in the First World War and to find a means of preventing such a catastrophe ever happening again. It ultimately proved a monumental failure. Even the very titles of books on the peace settlement of 1919 – *The economic consequences of the peace*, *The lost peace* and *The twenty year crisis* – reflect the fairly negative light in which the settlement has been viewed by historians.

What were the major difficulties facing the peacemakers in 1919?

A great number of difficult problems confronted the peacemakers. The previous European balance of power had been shattered by the bloody battles of the 'Great War'. The Russian Revolution of 1917 therefore aroused deep anxiety among the peacemakers concerning the possibility of a communist revolution spreading throughout Europe unless some new order were quickly established. In addition, Europe at the time of the peace conference was beset with deep economic problems, most notably a collapse of world trade, unstable currencies, unemployment, agricultural depression and mounting debts. Material damage inflicted during the First World War – devastated towns, railways and roads blown up, houses, farms and livestock destroyed, and merchant ships at the bottom of the sea – added to these economic worries. To complete a depressing picture, a flu epidemic spread across Europe in the months following the end of the war, claiming millions of lives.

Coping with the effects of war on this scale proved extremely difficult. A total of 17 million people were killed, severely wounded or permanently disabled in the conflict. This produced two different types of reaction among the victors and the vanquished. In the victorious countries, there were heated demands to 'make Germany pay' the economic costs of the war, while in the defeated nations, but particularly in Germany, movements of ex-soldiers emerged calling for vengeance. In Britain, the popular press screeched the banner headlines 'Squeeze the German lemon till the pips squeak' and 'Hang the Kaiser'.

What were the aims of the peacemakers?

All the major decisions at the conference were decided by the 'Council of Four' – the four major victorious Allies, represented in Paris by their respective leaders – David Lloyd George (Great Britain), **Woodrow Wilson** (USA), **Georges Clemenceau** (France) and Vittorio Orlando (Italy). The representatives of 28 other Allied nations were also present, but the Soviet Union, in diplomatic isolation, was not invited, and the defeated nations were required to accept the decisions of the peacemakers with little or no opportunity to modify them. The two major aims of the peacemakers were to bring political order to European politics and to prevent such a catastrophe ever happening again.

The four major victorious powers came to Paris with no agreed agenda, apart from Wilson's famous 14 points. The US president believed the war was due to three central causes – the secretive and selfish nature of European diplomacy, the tendency of larger powers to deny ethnic minorities **self-determination** and autocratic regimes which ignored the wishes of the people. Remove these three impediments to peace and a new order of international relations could be created, based on principles of open diplomacy, national self-determination and democracy. Such high moral principles seemed idealistic when compared to old-fashioned European diplomacy. However, Wilson proved less than completely faithful to his principles. There was very little democracy about the decision-making process. The Council of Four took all the decisions in closed sessions.

Clemenceau is often regarded as the chief architect of the harsh settlement with Germany. The French obsession with security at the conference was due to three factors – the long French frontier with Germany, the loss of Russia as a balance to German power in eastern Europe and the alarming differences in population and industrial potential between France and Germany. In fact, Clemenceau believed the gravest mistake of the peacemakers would be to make 'excessive demands' on Germany. The French desired two guarantees of future security against a possible German revival: first, the demilitarisation

Identify three difficulties facing the peacemakers.

Thomas Woodrow Wilson (1856–1924) was elected president of the USA in 1912, and was re-elected in 1916. Wilson's famous 14 points laid the basis for the signing of the armistice with Germany in November 1918. He gave strong support at the Paris peace settlement for the right of small nations to govern themselves and was a prime mover in the establishment of the League of Nations. He was bitterly disappointed when the US senate blocked US entry into the newly founded League. After a stroke in 1919, he decided to leave office.

Georges Clemenceau (1841–1929) was French prime minister from 1906 to 1909 and from 1917 to 1920. He played a leading role as a member of the 'Council of Four' in drafting the terms of the Paris peace settlement. He was passionately concerned with French security from further German aggression and is often viewed as the chief architect of the Treaty of Versailles. After being defeated in the 1920 presidential election, he retired from political life.

Self-determination is the right of a people or nation to choose their own system of government and elections, free of interference by outside powers.

The 'Big Three' at Versailles: Georges Clemenceau, Woodrow Wilson and David Lloyd George after signing the peace treaty.

Reparations are compensation for damage and injury suffered as a result of wilful acts of aggression (the term was applied to the requirement on Germany to pay the costs of the First World War).

of the region sandwiched between the German–French border, known as the Rhineland; and second, severe restrictions on German military power. In addition, the French sought financial assistance to rebuild their shattered territory. However, they pushed for a high **reparations** settlement only when their own demand for a cancellation of war debts was rejected by the USA and Britain. 'Every effort must be made to be just towards the Germans,' said Clemenceau, 'but when it comes to persuading them that we are just towards them, that is another matter.'

Lloyd George was primarily concerned to achieve a peace settlement which reconstructed Europe and ensured British involvement in European affairs was limited. The defeat of Germany had achieved all of Britain's war aims. The German naval threat was destroyed, the German military threat was seemingly defeated and the German colonial threat was over. This allowed Lloyd George to revert to the old idea of Britain taking a middle position within the European balance of power. As France was now the dominant military power, this meant taking a conciliatory attitude to Germany. As a result, the British delegation wanted military restrictions placed on Germany and some limited financial compensation, but not a totally punitive settlement. Many economic experts in the British delegation, including John Maynard Keynes, the brilliant young economist, saw German economic revival as vital for the recovery of Britain's European export trade and argued against a harsh reparations settlement.

Orlando, the Italian premier, was largely ignored by the three major powers, and proved ineffective. The Italian delegation wanted to gain territory as compensation for entering the war on the Allied side in 1915 and suffering heavy losses. But Orlando was unable to gain the port of Fiume, the prime territorial objective. The row over Fiume resulted in the Italian delegation walking out of the conference and led to the fall of Orlando's government. The denial of Fiume became a passionate nationalist issue in Italian politics. In 1919, Gabriele D'Annunzio, an Italian poet, formed a legion of nationalist agitators who seized the port and declared it a 'free city'. With problems at home and abroad, the Italian democratic government became deeply unpopular. It was eventually overthrown by Benito Mussolini, leader of the nationalist Fascist Party. During the inter-war period, 'fascism' became a popular and despotic alternative to weak democratic governments in a state of deep economic and political crisis in many parts of Europe.

Draw up a list of the major aims of Britain, the USA, France and Italy at the Peace Conference.

How fair was the Treaty of Versailles towards Germany?

Five separate treaties made up the Paris peace settlement, but the Treaty of Versailles, signed by Germany in the historic Hall of Mirrors at Versailles on 28 June 1919, was the most significant and controversial. German military power, the chief cause of the war, was the dominant issue at the peace conference. Germany had come very close to victory and most of its industry was untouched. Unless the peacemakers took adequate precautions, there was every prospect of a German revival. To prevent this, a number of arms limitations were implemented. The army was limited to 100,000 men, conscription abolished and tanks and aircraft prohibited. The navy was slimmed down to a coastal force of 36 vessels and the building of battleships and submarines was outlawed. By these measures, the German army was reduced to the level of that of Greece and the German navy was left on a par with that of Argentina.

Germany lost 13 per cent of its territory, including Alsace-Lorraine, Eupen-et-Malmédy, North Schleswig, West Prussia (the Polish Corridor) and Posen (Poznań). The loss of territory in eastern Europe was bitterly criticised by the German government. Danzig became a 'free city', linked by a customs union to the new Polish state, which also gained Upper Silesia, a major industrial area. The Poles were additionally given a 'corridor' of land to the sea, which cut off East Prussia from the rest of Germany. In western Europe, the French got what they wanted. The Rhineland was made a demilitarised zone and the Saar, a key coal-mining region, was placed under the control of the League of Nations. In

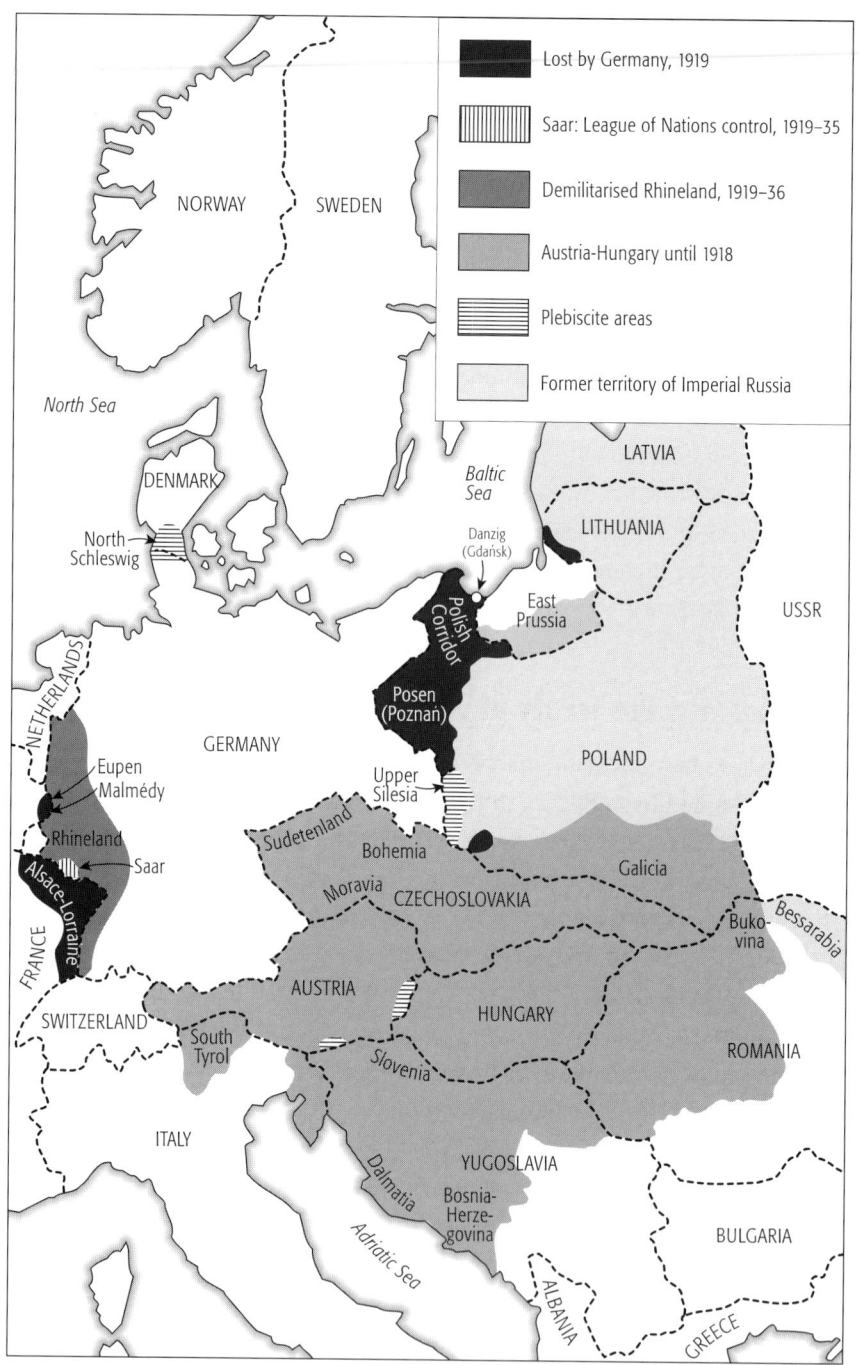

Map 2. Europe after the Paris peace settlement, 1919.

addition, all German colonies were put under League of Nations mandates and the Allies insisted that the German government agree to uphold a democratic constitution and free elections.

The Germans were also required to pay substantial financial compensation. The final figure, decided by the Reparations Committee in 1921, was set at £6,600 million, and all the foreign currency and assets of Germany abroad were seized. Not surprisingly, the German government thought the figure too high. To justify reparations, the Allies inserted article 231 into the treaty (the 'war guilt clause'), which obliged Germany to accept full responsibility for the outbreak of the war.

The German people greeted the terms of the Treaty of Versailles with varying degrees of anger, horror and disgust. The German leaders who signed the treaty were branded by nationalists as 'the criminals of 1919'. It is easy to understand the harsh reaction to the Treaty of Versailles in Germany. Most Germans had little idea of the size of the German defeat, and believed that, because Germany had requested an armistice, a lenient settlement would follow. As a result, the treaty came as an enormous shock. However, the loss of 13 per cent of its territory was much less harsh than France suffered at the Congress of Vienna in 1814–15, and far less punitive than the division of Germany after the Second World War. It was mild when compared with the Treaty of Brest-Litovsk. It is also possible to suggest that reparations were affordable, if only the German government had been really prepared to reduce living standards. In fact, the underlying economic and military potential of Germany remained favourable. Germany was surrounded by a number of weak powers in eastern Europe and faced no strong military alliance. Industry was modern, with a high level of skill in areas useful for armaments production. The German army was reduced, but its key strategists, the Prussian officer corps, remained. Germany had an excellent opportunity to pose a threat to Europe again. However, the *psychological* impact of the Treaty of Versailles on Germany was a much more important factor in subsequent events than its objective effects. Quite clearly, German people saw the treaty as harsh and blamed it for the social, economic and political ills of the Weimar regime. It is hard to deny that the Treaty of Versailles, lenient or otherwise, proved a very crucial rallying point for the revival of German nationalism, and the belief in its harshness also encouraged the British government to follow a policy of appeasement.

Briefly summarise the main restrictions placed on Germany under the terms of the Treaty of Versailles.

The other major treaties

The four other major treaties decided at Paris, which dealt with the other three defeated Central powers – Austria-Hungary (two treaties), Bulgaria and Turkey – also aroused criticism. The settlement of the territory of the former Austro-Hungarian Habsburg Empire was the most complex problem the peacemakers faced. The promise to ensure principles of national self-determination were applied to the widely diverse ethnic and national groups in central and eastern Europe proved extremely difficult to keep. Few ethnic groups were ever satisfied with the settlement in eastern Europe.

The Treaty of Trianon (1920) concerned Hungary and was arguably even harsher than the Treaty of Versailles. Hungary lost 66 per cent of its territory and 40 per cent of the ethnically diverse population of its former empire. Most of this territory went to Romania and Czechoslovakia.

The Treaty of St Germain (1919) dealt with Austria. All former territory of the Habsburg Empire, outside Austria, was shared between Czechoslovakia, which gained Bohemia and Moravia, including the Sudetenland with 4 million German-speakers; Italy, which took South Tyrol; Yugoslavia, which took Slovenia, Bosnia-Herzegovina and Dalmatia; Poland, which gained Galicia; and Romania, which was awarded Bukovina. The desire of Austria to unite with Germany was strictly forbidden.

Under the Treaty of Neuilly (1919), Bulgaria lost territory to Yugoslavia and Greece.

To further the principle of national self-determination, the peacemakers created two completely new states – Czechoslovakia and Yugoslavia. The historic state of Poland, carved out of German, Austrian and Russian territory, was also restored, but soon became a virtual military dictatorship. Yugoslavia, formed out of Serbia, with the addition of territory from Austria, Hungary and Bulgaria, was bitterly divided between the dominant Serbs and their Croat rivals and also lurched towards the right. Czechoslovakia, fashioned out of Austrian, Hungarian, Russian, Romanian and Polish territory, was the only fully functioning democracy in eastern Europe during the inter-war years. Even so, minority groups in Czechoslovakia claimed each coalition government was so dominated by the Czechs, who made up 65 per cent of the population, as to render the principle of national self-determination virtually meaningless.

The noble idea of national self-determination did not end traditional ethnic rivalries and disagreements. Eastern Europe was arguably more unstable and divided than ever before. The successor states of the former Habsburg Empire were weak, politically divided and in a poor economic condition, with little industry, weak currencies, inefficient agriculture, high debts and low investment. Falling world agricultural prices during the inter-war years ensured eastern Europe remained impoverished. The trading relations between the eastern European countries were stormy, owing to the use of protective tariffs.

What is more, parliamentary democracy never took root in eastern Europe. Hungary was deeply unstable and developed its own brand of fascist dictatorship in the 1930s. Austria was a political battleground between right and left, and parliamentary government gave way to right-wing dictatorship. Bulgaria and Romania also developed right-wing dictatorships, led by their respective

PEACE AND FUTURE CANNON FODDER

The Tiger : "Curious! I seem to hear a child weeping!"

Will Dyson's cartoon of 1919 shows the leaders of Britain, Italy, France and the USA leaving the Versailles peace conference. Clemenceau (The Tiger) looks towards a child of the '1940 class'. What concern is expressed by the cartoonist?

kings. Even among the three new states of eastern Europe, democracy was not in the ascendancy. The foreign relations of these eastern European states were also tense. In Hungary hatred was shown towards Czechoslovakia, Romania and Yugoslavia. The latter three powers responded by forming a close alliance in 1920, known as the 'Little Entente'. Polish–Czech relations were equally hostile, and the Yugoslav and Romanian governments disliked each other intensely. To add to the tension, the Soviet Union was locked in bitter territorial disputes with Poland and Romania, and the German government refused to accept the settlement of territory in eastern Europe. The only country in Europe which actively supported the new successor states was France, which signed treaties of mutual assistance with Poland (1921), Czechoslovakia (1924), Romania (1926) and Yugoslavia (1927). The French government hoped this group of eastern European powers, all committed to upholding the peace settlement in eastern Europe, might provide stability in the region. Yet these states, with their divided loyalties and discontented ethnic minorities, were no compensation for the loss of the Franco-Russian alliance.

The settlement of the territory of the former Ottoman Empire also produced tension and uncertainty. The Treaty of Sèvres (1920) divided Turkey into British, French and Italian spheres of influence and placed all former Ottoman possessions under British and French administration. However, a Turkish nationalist group (the Young Turks) gained power and chose to fight rather than accept the peace terms. This matter was finally resolved – after further haggling and small-scale military engagements – by the Treaty of Lausanne (1923), under which Turkey accepted its loss of colonies in return for a guarantee of territorial integrity.

Identify three major sources of conflict in eastern Europe which resulted from the Paris peace settlement.

How successful was the League of Nations in encouraging international co-operation from 1920 to 1933?

The League of Nations and the limits of international co-operation

The Paris peace conference also gave birth to the League of Nations, which was designed to create a completely new framework of international relations. The League had an agreed constitution, outlined in its Covenant, which pledged to 'respect and preserve against external aggression the territorial integrity and existing political independence of all members of the League', and to 'take action against any member regarded as an aggressor' through economic **sanctions** and, if these failed, 'collective military action'. The organisation consisted of an assembly, which met annually, a council, which had regular meetings and four permanent seats (Britain, Italy, France, Japan), raised to five, with the addition of Germany in 1926, and four temporary seats, elected by the assembly, raised to six in 1926 and nine in 1929. It was in the council that real power lay, but as each member had a veto over any decision there was not much real power to exercise. The day-to-day administration of the League was carried out by the secretariat. A permanent court of international justice was also established, at The Hague, to offer 'advisory opinions' on questions referred to it by the assembly or the council.

Sanctions are penalties, usually economic, used to place pressure on a nation to cease an act of aggression.

The League of Nations was a loose and flexible organisation, with members pledging to uphold an agreed set of principles set out in the Covenant. It faced a number of problems in establishing its authority. Defeated powers were denied entry until they proved a willingness to abide by the treaties imposed upon them. The original members were the 32 Allied powers and 12 additional neutral states. A 'victors' club' was how the League was viewed in Germany. A 'capitalist club' was how the Soviet Union, also denied entry, described the new organisation. But the biggest blow of all to the early credibility of the League was the decision of the US senate to block US entry. This deprived the League of one of its key architects and the most powerful non-European power. In reality, the League was largely a European club, dominated by the victorious powers. Very few European diplomats thought the League of Nations would replace the self-interests of each nation-state.

During the 1920s the League enjoyed mixed success as an effective peace-keeper. On the one hand, a few minor disputes were settled by the League, most notably the withdrawal of Yugoslav troops from Albania and the resolution of a territorial dispute over the Åland islands, between Finland and Sweden. Successful **arbitration** was achieved in disputes between Germany and Poland over Upper Silesia, Britain and Turkey over the administration of oil fields in Mosul, and between Greece and Bulgaria over disputed territory in the Balkans. On the other hand, the League could not prevent Poland annexing Vilnius in 1922, Italians occupying Corfu in 1923 or stop the war between Bolivia and Paraguay in the early 1930s.

An even more worrying development was the complete failure of the Geneva Protocol, which had been designed to commit all League members to engage in collective military action in the event of acts of unprovoked aggression. France was a keen supporter of the idea, but it was vetoed by Austen Chamberlain, the British foreign secretary, in March 1925. The British believed the Geneva Protocol would turn the League into a 'policeman of the world' and involve Britain in all manner of minor and major disputes.

However, the League of Nations did promote a greater level of international co-operation than had ever existed before. This climate encouraged the signing by Britain, Japan, France, Italy and the USA of the Washington naval agreement in 1922, which set limits on naval shipbuilding, and the 1930 London naval agreement signed by Britain, Japan, Italy and the USA, which set limits on submarines and the scrapping of some warships. This same spirit encouraged the signing by 15 major powers in August 1928 of the Kellogg–Briand Pact, which pledged all its signatories to reject 'war as an instrument of national policy' and promised to settle disputes between nations by 'pacific means'. By 1933, 60 nations had made this pledge, very much in the spirit of the Covenant of the League of Nations.

The biggest disappointment of the League in this period was its total failure to achieve a reduction in armaments. The world disarmament conference, organised by the League, opened in 1932, and was attended by 61 nations and 5 non-members, including the USA and the Soviet Union. The chief aim was to set agreed limits on army, air-force and naval weapons. A French idea for a League of Nations army was rejected. A proposal by the British government to place limits on 'offensive' weapons, including tanks, bomber aircraft, submarines, poison gas and chemical weapons, also floundered. More alarmingly,

Arbitration is the settlement of disputes through the adjudication of an impartial third party.

the German and Soviet delegations refused to accept a resolution passed by 41 votes to prohibit air attacks, the use of tanks and chemical weapons. The German delegation constantly argued for 'equality of rights' and demanded the other powers either disarm to the German level imposed at Versailles or allow Germany to rearm to the level of other major powers. The German delegation walked out, and agreed to return only if Germany was given equal treatment.

Non-European problems

The way the peacemakers dealt with non-European problems left a great deal to be desired. A demand by Japan to have a clause proclaiming a commitment to 'racial equality' placed in the Covenant of the League of Nations was rejected. Nationalist groups who demanded the right to self-determination in the Middle East, Africa and India were politely informed the principle would not apply to them. In fact, imperial rule was actually expanded at the Paris peace conference. All former Turkish and German colonies were termed 'mandated territories' and placed under the supervision of the victorious powers. The British Empire assumed control of the former Ottoman territories of Palestine, Iraq, Transjordan and the former German African colonies of Togoland and the Cameroon. The French gained control over Syria and Libya and were allowed access to oil in Mosul, Iraq. The fig leaf of a League of Nations mandate hid old-fashioned imperial gains. British and French offi-

THE DOORMAT.

A 1933 cartoon by David Low criticising the actions of Japan and the ineffectiveness of the League of Nations.

cials claimed they were marching the mandated territories towards independence, but nationalist groups doubted if such a day would ever arrive.

The disposal of the former German colonies in the Asia–Pacific region served only to inflame relations between China and Japan still further. China had entered the war on the side of the Allies in 1917 and expected to regain control of former German colonies in Africa and Asia on the principle of national self-determination. However, Japan, an ally of Britain since 1902, seized these areas in 1914 and expected to retain them. The peacemakers decided Japan would keep its trading rights in Manchuria and Inner Mongolia, but would not gain political control. It was also decided that Japan should supervise the administration of Shantung, provided they promised to return the area to China at a future date. This settlement satisfied neither Japan nor China and laid the basis for a long-running and bitter dispute between the two nations, which eventually led to full-scale war in 1937.

> What criticisms can be made of how the peacemakers dealt with non-European problems?

Historical interpretation: the 1919 peace settlement

A great many historians have viewed the 1919 peace settlement as a failed compromise between the idealism of Wilson, the US president, and the realism and selfishness of the European powers. As James Joll puts it, 'Europe was divided by the peace conference into those who wanted the peace revised (Germany, Italy, Japan and Hungary), those who wanted it upheld (France, Poland, Czechoslovakia and Yugoslavia) and those who were not that interested (USA and Britain)'.

For E. H. Carr the Paris peace settlement was based on unworkable idealistic principles, most notably national self-determination and **collective security**, but the fundamental weakness of the settlement was its failure to solve the 'German problem'. This view was supported by A. J. P. Taylor, who suggested the Treaty of Versailles was crushing, vindictive and lacked moral validity because 'no German accepted it as a fair settlement and all Germans wanted to shake it off'. For Taylor, the Second World War was really 'a war over the settlement of Versailles; a war which had been implicit when the First World War ended because the peacemakers had not solved the "German problem"'. The failure of the peace settlement to create a viable balance of power in Europe has been seen as a vital weakness. In P. M. H. Bell's view, the peace settlement was 'a rickety edifice wh[...] unstable from the start'. At the heart of its weak foundations [...] Anthony Lentin's view, a failure to tackle the underlying potential [...] many. The peacemakers did not seem to realise the collapse of Ru[...] the Habsburg and Ottoman Empires left Germany in a potentially [...] position in Europe than ever before. The newly constituted nati[...]

> **Collective security** describes the maintenance of peace through the combined effort of a group of powers.

The Paris peace settlement and its aftermath, 191[...]

of central and eastern Europe were small, weak, ethnically divided and open to domination by a resurgent Germany.

However, many historians offer a much more sympathetic interpretation of the Paris peace settlement. Adam Adamthwaite views the peace settlement as a 'brave attempt to deal with intractable, perhaps insoluble problems'. For Ruth Henig, the settlement was 'a creditable achievement', which failed because of the severe economic and social problems left behind by the war, major divisions among the peacemakers about the terms of the settlement and, most importantly, the reluctance of political leaders in the inter-war period to enforce it. According to this view, the architects of the peace settlement failed to follow through the principles laid down in Paris; their failure ensured a German revival and, through further doses of indecisiveness, brought about war.

Paul Birdsall views the refusal of the USA to become involved in upholding the settlement as a crucial reason for its subsequent failure. This destroyed the prospects of building a successful League of Nations and the forging of a democratic front to uphold the settlement. Paul Kennedy points out the great differences between the success of the settlement in the 1920s, when it worked, and its shortcomings during the 1930s, when it was crushed by the combined militarism of Germany, Japan and Italy. For Kennedy, the crucial reason for its collapse was the Great Depression of the early 1930s, which destroyed international co-operation and encouraged extreme selfishness to dominate international relations. The Depression also helped destroy German democracy, and contributed to the rise of Adolf Hitler.

Summary questions

1 Identify and explain at least *two* reasons why Germany was dissatisfied with the Treaty of Versailles.

2 Identify and explain the major aims of the peacemakers.

ich was

was, in

of Ger-

ssia and

stronger

on-states

5 Italy, 1919–45: the rise and fall of Mussolini and fascism

Significant dates

1915   Italy enters the First World War

1919   The Italian government plays a leading role at the Paris peace conference, but is dissatisfied with its failure to gain more territory

1919   *September*   D'Annunzio seizes Fiume

1921   *November*   The Fascist Party (PNF) is established

1922   *October*   Mussolini leads march on Rome and is offered post of prime minister in coalition government
       December   Fascist grand council established

1923   Italy seizes Corfu

1924   Italy gains formal control of Fiume
       June   Murder of Matteotti leads to a walk-out from parliament of socialist members

1925   *January*   Mussolini declares Italy a 'dictatorship'

1926   Ministry of corporations set up

1929   Concordat signed between Mussolini and the Vatican

1935   *October*   Italy invades Abyssinia (modern-day Ethiopia)

1936   *July*   Mussolini sends Italian troops to fight with the nationalists in the Spanish Civil War
       October   Rome–Berlin Axis signed by Mussolini and Hitler

1938   Racial laws enacted

1939	*April* Italy annexes Albania
	May Pact of Steel between Germany and Italy is signed
	September Outbreak of Second World War. Italy remains neutral
1940	*June* Italy enters the Second World War as an ally of Germany
1943	*July* Mussolini is ousted from power
	September Italy surrenders to the Allies
1945	*April* Mussolini is killed by communist partisans and his body is displayed hanging upside down from a lamp-post in Milan

Overview

The ordeal of the First World War left Italy in a state of turmoil. Over 500,000 Italian troops were killed, with another million wounded, and many left permanently disabled. From 1918 to 1922, there were five different coalition governments, none of which proved popular with the Italian people. There were strikes, and pitched street battles between the socialists and right-wing nationalists, known as the Fascists, led by Benito Mussolini. The Italian middle classes increasingly demanded a strong government to deal with the revolutionary unrest in Italy during the immediate post-war years. In October 1922, after a prolonged period of strikes, riots and civil unrest, Mussolini's Fascist Party marched to Rome in protest against the continual disruption and industrial unrest in Italian society, and, with the agreement of King Victor Emmanuel III, Mussolini took power. Italy was the first major European nation to follow **fascism** during the inter-war period. This chapter examines the rise and fall of Mussolini's brand of fascism in Italy from 1919 to 1945.

What is fascism?

Fascism had an enormous impact in a number of European countries during the first half of the twentieth century. As a result, it is useful to define what the term 'fascism' actually means. It is applied not only to Italy under Mussolini from 1922 to 1945, but also to Germany under Hitler from 1933 to 1945, and to many other right-wing regimes, including the rule of Franco in Spain. Of course, 'fascist' regimes differed from place to place, but they did have some basic similarities. There was a strong emphasis in fascist ideology on nationalism and on the absolute power of the state. Fascism always portrayed itself as the enemy of, and a popular rival to, the mass appeal of socialism and communism, as well as liberal democracy. Most fascist regimes had, or claimed to have had, a **totalitarian** type of government which attempted to control the life of the individual. All fascist regimes had powerful leaders as their

Fascism was a political philosophy and a system of government which became popular in Europe, especially during the inter-war period. Fascism was nationalistic and authoritarian, but also claimed to be a radical 'third way' between democracy and communism.

Totalitarian describes a system of government which attempts to gain total control over society and which allows no rival parties or rival viewpoints to those expressed by the ruling elite or party.

figure-head. Most were one-party states, with no opposition parties, no free trade unions and no democratic elections. Fascism also laid great emphasis on military strength.

In economic policy, most fascist regimes supported the interests of big business, imposed taxes on imports of foreign goods, and followed policies aimed at economic self-sufficiency. Another feature of fascist regimes was the control of the mass media in order to project an image of the leader as a popular figure. Mussolini claimed Italian fascism was 'anti-communist' and opposed to an 'economic conception' of the development of history. Mussolini also argued that fascism was opposed to democratic and liberal ideology. According to Mussolini, fascism viewed the power of the state as 'absolute'.

> Identify three of the major characteristics of a fascist regime.

Why did fascism develop in Italy after the First World War?

The problems of Italian democracy before 1914

The Italian state, a constitutional monarchy created in 1871, was deeply unstable from the very beginning. Before 1914, a stable democracy had failed to take root. No single party ever commanded a majority in parliament. Party labels did not seem to matter at all in Italian politics. As a result, coalition governments, usually consisting of combinations of 'liberals' and 'conservatives', depended on finding a consensus on key issues. There were 31 different governments between 1860 and 1914. The result was paralysis at the heart of Italian democracy.

Italy was also beset by sharp differences between the prosperous and fashionable north and the poverty-stricken and agricultural south. The Catholic Church refused to co-operate with the Italian government. Indeed, until 1904, Catholics were told by the Vatican not to vote in Italian elections. In addition, there was industrial unrest and strong political differences between the nationalist right and the growing socialist movement.

The impact of the First World War

At the beginning of the First World War, the Italian government had opted for neutrality. After much persuasion from the Allies, Italy decided to enter the war in 1915 in the hope of gaining territorial concessions. However, Italy suffered over half a million dead. There was great disappointment throughout the country over the minimal gains achieved by the Italian government at the Paris peace conference. The peacemakers gave Italy only limited territory in south Tyrol, Istria, Trieste and part of Albania. As a result, the sense of outrage in Italy that the war had been fought in vain was strong, especially among frustrated ex-soldiers. The romantic poet Gabriele D'Annunzio denounced the moderate Liberal government for bringing 'a mutilated victory'. In an act of defiance against the peace settlement, D'Annunzio occupied Fiume in 1919, with a makeshift band of less than 2,000 renegade nationalists. He was applauded as a nationalist hero on the right, but his occupation ended in 1920 when it was put down by Italian troops after 15 months.

Economic and political instability

Another consequence of war was to leave Italy in a very poor economic condition. There was high inflation, a mountain of unpaid war debts, high unemployment, severe agricultural depression, which hit farmers in the south extremely hard, and a collapse in the value of the lira. The result was a severe fall in the standard of living of Italian people, and a growing disillusionment with the parliamentary system.

The introduction of proportional representation in 1919, which allowed small parties to gain seats in parliament, made the already unstable political system in Italy even more open to manipulation. There was even less consistency or agreement in the implementation of policies than had been the case before 1914. As a result, democracy in Italy was less popular after 1918. Those groups opposed to fascism in Italy, in particular communists and socialists, were engaged in disagreements with each other, which ensured they failed to unite against the threat posed to democracy by right-wing nationalism.

Industrial and agricultural unrest

In addition, there was severe industrial and agricultural unrest in the immediate aftermath of the First World War. A wave of strikes occurred between 1918 and 1920, which often brought industry and transport to a complete standstill. In many cases, workers occupied factories, while in the countryside there was a series of 'land occupations' by peasants who seized land from landlords or large farmers. By the end of 1921, there were 3.5 million peasant farmers, all trying to make a living in a period when agricultural prices were falling sharply.

Briefly outline three problems facing Italian democracy immediately after the end of the First World War.

In the cities, the level of unrest was equally alarming. In 1920, for example, there were 1,800 strikes, and worker occupations of factories became commonplace. In the immediate post-war period, therefore, Italy seemed on the verge of revolution or civil war. Not surprisingly, leading industrialists, farmers and army leaders called for a strong government to curb the chaos in Italian politics and society.

The rise of Mussolini and the growth of the Fascist Party
Mussolini

It was within this deeply unstable political and economic environment that Italian fascism grew and prospered. The Fascist movement was founded in

1919 by Benito Mussolini, who was born in Romagna in 1883 (the son of a blacksmith father and a schoolteacher mother). In the early stage of his political development, Mussolini was a socialist journalist, who edited a leading left-wing newspaper (*Avanti*). He was an outspoken critic before the First World War of military aggression and opposed Italian participation in it. However, his experiences as a soldier during the First World War, and his dissatisfaction with the political unrest in Italy that it provoked, helped to push Mussolini towards the nationalist right. Mussolini's greatest skill was in adapting his incoherent Fascist ideology to gain popular support from a wide section of the Italian population. He offered the promise of stability within a political system which seemed chaotic. This had a powerful appeal in a period of deep crisis.

The growth of the Fascist Party

In 1919, Mussolini established the Fasci di Combattimento, paramilitary squads of ex-soldiers (dubbed 'fighting groups') who became well known in their distinctive black shirts for engaging in violent attacks on strikers in cities, and for engaging in violence with socialist groups in the countryside. Indeed, Mussolini's Fascist squads gained notoriety for their violence against socialists rather than for any notable set of new policies. In 1921, Mussolini decided to turn his combat group into an official political party: the Fascist Party (Partito Nazionale Fascista – PNF), which gained 35 seats in the Italian parliament during the elections in 1921.

Mussolini's promise to rescue Italy from 'feeble government' struck a chord with big business and the Church (which saw him as a vital anti-communist weapon), and also drew support from property owners in the middle classes in cities and in certain rural areas who longed for a return to stability. The Fascist Party also found sympathy from within the Italian army. Mussolini was viewed by all these groups as a guarantor of law and order.

Between 1921 and 1922, membership of the Fascist Party grew rapidly, from 3,000 to 300,000. Support for the party came largely from ex-soldiers, students, the middle classes in cities and more affluent members of rural communities. The party was weakest among agricultural workers in the south and working-class industrial workers in the cities. Italian Fascism was a revolt of the middle class against the rise of socialism and trade union power.

Identify the key reasons for the growth of the Fascist Party in Italy.

Mussolini's rise to power

The Italian government started to become reliant on Fascist squads to put down strikes. In July 1922, for example, the Fascist Party played a crucial role in helping the army to put down the general strike. Following this success, Mussolini started to demand a leading role for the Fascist Party in the coalition

Mussolini (centre) marches on Rome in October 1922.

government as a reward for helping to quell left-wing unrest. The industrialists began to give the Fascists financial support, which greatly enhanced the national standing of the party. In May 1921, Giovanni Giolitti, the prime minister, decided to include the Fascist Party in a new coalition, dubbed the 'National Bloc'. This added to the growing acceptance of the Fascist Party among the ruling elite of Italian politics. Large sections of the army and the police were also supportive of Mussolini's determination to take a strong stand against socialists and trade union members who were engaged in industrial unrest.

In August 1922, the socialists organised another general strike as a counter-attack against the growing nationalism of the Italian government. This gave Mussolini the opportunity to portray the Fascist Party as the only barrier in the way of a communist take-over. In October 1922, Mussolini led 50,000 of his black shirts on a march to Rome (Mussolini actually went by train) with the aim of seizing power. By this time, Victor Emmanuel III had already decided to invite Mussolini to form a coalition government on his arrival. When Mussolini did arrive, the police and the army stood aside. Mussolini was immediately invited by the king to form a government. The king could have used the army and the police to attack the black shirts, but he chose not to do so.

There are a number of reasons why Mussolini came to power in 1922.

1 The king believed it made sense to bring Mussolini's violent group into the government rather than to create further division within the right of Italian society, which might have provoked a bitter civil war.

2 The Italian establishment, especially factions within the army, big business and the Catholic Church, was willing to stand aside and allow Mussolini to establish a strong authoritarian government in order to weaken the power of organised labour and communism.

3 The elevation of Mussolini to power was due to the prolonged economic and social problems in Italy since the end of the First World War. The ruling elite in Italy felt Mussolini might be able to establish a strong government which would bring stability. By the end of 1922, Mussolini's dynamic leadership seemed to the ruling elite a better alternative to the tired and unstable coalitions which had ruled Italy in the immediate post-war period.

How did Mussolini consolidate his political power in Italy from 1922 to 1928?

The movement towards **dictatorship** and a one-party state in Italy developed in stages. From 1922 to 1924, Mussolini was the prime minister of a coalition government, including Fascists, Nationalists and some Conservatives. With a mixture of compromise with the king, big business, the army and the Church, sprinkled with violence towards his opponents, Mussolini was able to transform Italy into a one-party state.

The electoral law was altered in 1924 so that the leading coalition grouping – which turned out to be Mussolini's Fascist Party and his supporters – were given 66 per cent of parliamentary seats. This greatly enhanced Mussolini's position as prime minister. The suppression of democracy was denounced by Socialists in the Italian parliament. Giacomo Matteotti, a young Socialist deputy, called the 1924 election a 'sham'. In June 1924, Matteotti was kidnapped by Fascists and stabbed to death. For the rest of the year, the 'Matteotti crisis' looked likely to bring about the fall of Mussolini, who was held responsible by the left for the murder of the young Socialist idealist. However, the opponents of Mussolini in parliament, composed of Socialists and Populists, decided to withdraw from parliament in protest against the murder. They hoped that this boycott of parliament would encourage Victor Emmanuel III to dismiss Mussolini from office. But the king refused to bow to opposition pressure to sack the Fascist leader.

As a result, Mussolini remained in power and was able to consolidate his rule over Italy. In January 1925, he gained an agreement from the king which

Dictatorship is rule by a single powerful figure, supported by either a single party or the armed forces and usually by both.

enabled him to enact law without the agreement of parliament. This allowed him to ban all the political parties, except the Fascist Party, to introduce strict censorship of the press, to ban the trade unions, to appoint Fascist officials to run local government, and to increase the powers of the police and army to arrest political opponents and crush rebellion. In 1928, a second new electoral law restricted the choice of voters in elections to a single list of candidates (all Fascist) who were chosen by Mussolini and the Fascist grand council.

By these means, Italy became a one-party state led by Mussolini, who adopted the title of Il Duce (The Leader). It is important to stress, however, that Mussolini wielded power as the dictatorial head of the existing state machinery, and his rule relied on the support both of the king, who retained the power to dismiss Mussolini, and of the army, the police, big business and the Church. Indeed, the independent power of the Fascist Party was extremely limited. As a result, Mussolini had to share power with these interest groups, which he always feared might challenge his authority. Consequently, he did not create a totalitarian regime in which there were no individuals or groups not controlled by the state. Hannah Arendt describes Italy under Mussolini as a 'nationalistic dictatorship' rather than a 'totalitarian' regime which exerted total power over society. In the view of A. J. P. Taylor, Mussolini was 'a Sawdust Caesar', whose power was based more on propaganda myth than on reality.

> Briefly summarise how Mussolini consolidated his power over Italy.

How successful were Mussolini's domestic and foreign policies?

Relations with the Church

Mussolini had no strong religious beliefs, but he was keen to promote cordial relations with the Catholic Church. In February 1929, therefore, he signed a concordat with the pope which established Catholicism as the sole religion of the Italian people and made the Vatican City independent. In return, the Vatican recognised the Kingdom of Italy. The concordat was Mussolini's most enduring domestic reform, because it healed over 50 years of hostility between church and state, and greatly increased the popularity of the Fascist regime with many Catholics.

Relations between Mussolini and the Vatican did become strained in the late 1930s, however, when the Italian dictator (influenced by Hitler) started to introduce anti-Semitic legislation which banned Jews from the professions, business and the army. Pope Pius XI condemned these anti-Semitic laws, which were also strongly opposed and ignored by a large number of Italians. It was only when the Nazis took control of northern Italy in 1943 that Jews started to suffer large-scale persecution.

Economic policy

The corporate state

The most significant economic reform carried out by Mussolini was the creation of the 'corporate state'. The idea was to end conflict between capital and labour. In principle, **corporatism** involved greater government control over industry, without destroying private enterprise. In practice, the system favoured business over labour. By 1934, a total of 22 corporations had been established to control industries such as steel, textiles, coal, shipping, electricity, iron, telephones and wine production. By 1940, the Italian government held a 20 per cent stake in industry, which was higher than in any other European country except the communist Soviet Union. Fascism in Italy favoured heavy industries such as coal, steel, transport and armaments over consumer industries.

It was hoped that the corporate state would bring more planning to the Italian economy, and help to promote good relations between employers and employees. In practice, the corporations were dominated by the employers and operated in their interests. The rights of workers were severely curtailed, with strikes banned and unions prohibited. Workers also suffered a series of national pay cuts in 1927, 1930 and 1934. The corporate state did help established industries, but did not bring any dramatic improvement in Italy's long-standing economic problems. On the contrary, greater state interference in private industry increased red tape and was resented by many enterprising business people.

The economy

Apart from the idea of the corporate state, Mussolini's regime did not apply any consistent set of economic policies. Between 1922 and 1929, a traditional liberal policy of balancing the budget was followed, which helped industry and agriculture to expand. A more damaging economic policy supported by Mussolini was to set the value of the lira at a very high level against the pound, which increased the price of many Italian exports, and helped to reduce the overseas sales of cars and textiles. It was only in 1936 that Mussolini realised this error and finally devalued the lira.

Another economic policy followed by Mussolini was a drive for national self-sufficiency, which was designed to make the Italian economy less dependent on imports. High tariffs were imposed on foreign imports, which were designed to protect industry, and the government also provided industry with loans and subsidies to improve productivity.

The most significant attempt at self-sufficiency by Mussolini's regime was the much trumpeted 'Battle for Grain', which did cut imports of wheat by 75 per cent between 1925 and 1935. However, this fall in grain imports was

Corporatism is an attempt to combine elements of state control and capitalist enterprise and which tries to bring harmony between the managers and workers.

achieved only at the expense of weakening the production of other crops and weakening the dairy industry.

By and large, Fascist economic policies were extremely unsuccessful. Self-sufficiency was never achieved, even in agriculture. The budget, which was balanced in the 1920s, was in deficit by the late 1930s. Unemployment remained over 1 million for most of the 1930s and inflation was over 20 per cent. The wages of workers in industry and agriculture also declined from 1922 to 1939.

Identify three major domestic reforms introduced by the Fascist regime.

Propaganda

The key aspect of Mussolini's rule in Italy was effective propaganda. Indeed, Denis Mack Smith argues that Mussolini's greatest skill lay in projecting himself through propaganda as a 'superman'. By these means, Mussolini attempted to divert attention from the inefficiency of the regime, and to give the misleading impression abroad that Italy was a much greater military power than was actually the case. The mass media were used to project the image of Mussolini as a dynamic action man, even though he was balding (he later shaved his whole head), of average height, short-sighted and suffered from crippling pains due to stomach ulcers. Mussolini has been described by Denis Mack

A propaganda photograph intending to show how fit Fascist leaders were.

Smith as a 'stupendous poseur'. Slogans on posters such as 'Mussolini is always right' added to the prevailing propaganda myth of his power over the Italian people. However, the presentation of Mussolini as a 'superman' actually led the Italian dictator to believe in his own publicity, and led him into a disastrous close relationship with Adolf Hitler.

Education

Mussolini wanted to use the existing education system as a means of indoctrinating the young with Fascist ideas. Yet the process of Fascist indoctrination in schools was extremely slow. It was only in 1936 that textbooks which had been approved by Mussolini's regime were introduced in schools. From 1938, anti-Semitic ideas were taught in many schools. However, Fascist indoctrination was not effectively implemented. There was resistance in many Catholic schools and especially within the university sector, which remained largely free of Fascist indoctrination. The many Fascist youth groups which Mussolini set up, such as Balila, the Avanguardisti and the Fascist Levy, were far less popular than, for example, the Hitler Youth was in Nazi Germany. In fact, 40 per cent of children between 8 and 18 years never joined any of the Fascist youth organisations from 1931 to 1939.

Foreign and colonial policy

Mussolini hoped to make a significant impact on European affairs. He was also concerned to expand the Italian colonial empire. As a result, he engaged in a number of major foreign policy initiatives and some important colonial adventures in the inter-war years.

Mussolini was determined to improve Italy's international position by increasing Italian diplomatic power in Europe and the Mediterranean. Closely linked to this objective was his desire to expand Italy's small colonial empire in Africa. As a result, his foreign policy alternated between acts of conciliation on the European diplomatic scene and acts of aggression in the colonial sphere.

Mussolini had always believed Italy had not received enough territory at the Paris peace conference, and he often took aggressive actions to rectify this perceived injustice in his colonial policy. In October 1923, for example, Italy seized the Greek island of Corfu and demanded 50 million lira from the Greek government. This high-handed action was followed in 1924 by a negotiated agreement with the Yugoslavian government, which allowed the urban area of Fiume to be incorporated into Italy. In 1926, Mussolini declared a protectorate over Albania. At the same time, Italy secured control of some small pieces of territory in Africa. But these small territorial gains in the colonial sphere fell way short of Mussolini's long-term ambition of creating a large north African empire for Italy.

It was, however, during the 1930s that Mussolini made his most significant impact on European and colonial affairs. In 1930, he declared that Italy would expand its armed forces, and revise treaties which prohibited Italian colonial expansion. When Hitler came to power in 1933, however, Mussolini had no intention of building close relations with Nazi Germany. On the contrary, he had good relations with Britain and France and was a strong defender of Austrian independence. Indeed, Mussolini believed Italy could act as a mediator between the growth of German power on the one hand and the aims of British and French diplomacy on the other. In July 1934, when the Austrian leader Engelbert Dollfuss was assassinated by pro-Nazi thugs, Mussolini sent Italian troops to the Austrian border, which helped to force Hitler to publicly declare he had no interest in seizing Austria. In March 1935, when Hitler announced German rearmament, Mussolini joined the leaders of Britain and France at Stresa in April to denounce German actions.

The great turning point in Mussolini's foreign policy came in October 1935, when Italy invaded Abyssinia. The reasons why he decided to engage in this act of unprovoked aggression at a time of great international tension were difficult to understand at the time, but it did fit in with his desire to expand Italy's meagre colonial empire. It also seems likely that Mussolini believed the conquest of Abyssinia would increase the popularity of his regime during a period when the Italian economy was in the doldrums. He thought that the British and French governments, who were preoccupied with the growth of Nazi Germany, would not take any action against Italian aggression towards a small African power, out of fear that he might move closer to Hitler. What Mussolini did not calculate was the high level of public outrage about his colonial policy, especially in Britain and France. Economic sanctions were imposed on Italy through the League of Nations. The British and French governments, however, did seek a compromise with Mussolini over Abyssinia, which served to worsen matters. In December 1935, Samuel Hoare, the British foreign secretary, and Pierre Laval, the French foreign minister, met in Paris and cobbled together a secret deal (the Hoare–Laval Pact), which agreed that Mussolini should be allowed to retain 75 per cent of Abyssinia. When news leaked out of this cloak-and-dagger deal, it caused deep embarrassment and led to the resignations of both Hoare and Laval. As a result, the League of Nations was discredited and was no longer considered an effective peace-keeper.

Even worse, Mussolini drew closer to Hitler and Nazi Germany in the aftermath of the Abyssinian affair. Hitler had not criticised the Italian invasion and sought to develop close relations with Italy afterwards. The two countries collaborated together in aiding General Franco's nationalists in the Spanish Civil War from 1936 to 1939. Another sign of closer German–Italian relations was the formation of the Rome–Berlin axis of Europe's two major fascist powers, in October 1936. Italy also joined the anti-Comintern Pact with Germany and Japan in 1937, which pledged to stop the world-wide spread of communism. In March 1938, Mussolini dropped his opposition to Hitler's desire to unite Germany with Austria. This proved a significant factor in encouraging Hitler to occupy Austria.

However, not all of Mussolini's interventions in foreign policy were aggressive and disruptive. He did make a significant contribution to preventing war in September 1938, when he helped to persuade Hitler to sign the Munich agreement, which was intended to prevent a European war breaking out over the issue of minority rights for German-speakers in the Sudeten region of Czechoslovakia. Indeed, the Munich agreement greatly increased Mussolini's popularity in Italy and enhanced his supposed 'superman' status.

Mussolini's period as a 'good European', however, did not last very long. In April 1939 he heightened European tension once more by ordering the invasion of Albania. In May 1939, Italy signed a military alliance (the 'Pact of Steel') with Hitler. When the Second World War broke out in September 1939, however, Mussolini, realising Italy's power was more talk than reality, decided Italy would be a 'non-belligerent'. If Mussolini had kept out of the Second World War, his regime, like that of Franco in Spain, might have survived. As it was, he decided to cement his 'brutal friendship' with Hitler into a stronger alliance. By choosing Germany as an ally, Mussolini effectively signed up as the junior partner in Hitler's grandiose plans to dominate Europe. As a result, Italy could no longer act as a mediator in European affairs. Indeed, his own survival became bound up with the success of the German army.

> Assess the major aspects of Mussolini's foreign policy.

What were the consequences for Italy of involvement in the Second World War?

In June 1940, Mussolini decided Italy would enter the Second World War on Hitler's side. With France defeated, he believed Hitler was on course for ultimate victory in Europe. This miscalculation proved fatal. Italy was not militarily prepared for a conflict with the British Empire in north Africa and the Mediterranean. The position of Italy deteriorated even further after the entry of the USA into the conflict at the end of 1941. By early 1943, British and American forces had driven the Italian and German forces out of Africa. By the summer of 1943, they had mounted a successful invasion of southern Italy, meeting with very little military resistance.

In July 1943, Mussolini was dismissed from power by the king. The new Italian government signed an armistice with the Allies, while Nazi Germany responded by mounting an invasion of northern Italy. Mussolini, who had

THE DREAM AND THE NIGHTMARE

A David Low cartoon, from the *Evening Standard*, 11 June 1940, produced when Mussolini decided Italy should go to war.

been put under house arrest by the king, was helped to escape from prison by an enterprising German army squad. He was placed by Hitler at the head of a Nazi puppet regime (the Salo Republic) in northern Italy. In April 1945, the Allies finally occupied northern Italy. Mussolini was captured by Italian partisans and executed. His body and that of his partner, Clara Petacci, were hung upside down in a public thoroughfare in Milan. This was the ignominious end which befell Europe's first fascist dictator, whose regime had become deeply unpopular ever since Italy had entered the Second World War.

There are several reasons why Italy suffered such a swift and catastrophic defeat in the Second World War:

1 Mussolini's decision to join Germany in 1940 made Italy dependent on German success.
2 Mussolini did not consider the implications for Italy when the Soviet Union in June 1941 and the USA in December 1941 entered the war.
3 Italy's armed forces were not prepared to meet the demands placed upon them in fighting war in Europe and Africa.

Underlying Italy's weak armed forces was a limited industrial base. As a result, military defeats for Italy were inevitable and provoked a storm of dissatisfaction with Mussolini's regime inside Italy. In the final analysis, Italian Fascism perished on the ego of Mussolini and his totally mistaken belief that Italy could become a first-rank European power, with the help of Hitler, during the Second World War.

Identify two reasons for the fall of Mussolini during the Second World War.

Historical interpretation: Mussolini and the road to war

The historical debate over Mussolini's Fascist Italy has concentrated on the nature of Mussolini's rule inside Italy from 1922 to 1945 and Italy's role in the origins of the Second World War.

Most historians now agree that Mussolini never made Italy a totalitarian state. He was more successful in projecting himself as a powerful and popular leader through misleading propaganda than his regime was in creating a coherent system of government or developing any success in economic or social affairs. As a result, Denis Mack Smith views Mussolini's Fascist regime as confused and inefficient, and one which left no lasting achievements. Hannah Arendt views Fascist Italy as a much less totalitarian and repressive regime than either Hitler's Germany and Stalin's Soviet Union. Mussolini's economic policies have been viewed as largely window dressing for the dominance of big business over organised labour. However, Ian Kershaw has recently argued that there were some similarities between the aims of Hitler and Mussolini in many areas of domestic policy. Both fascist leaders wanted to destroy the power of organised labour, both wanted to adopt aggressive foreign policies, and both furthered the aims of the army and monopolistic forms of industry. On the other hand, many other historians have stressed major differences between Hitler's and Mussolini's domestic policies, especially racial policy. Mussolini was not a firm supporter of Hitler's racial ideology, and he adopted anti-Semitic laws in Italy, which were not popular with the Italian people, only to curry favour with Hitler rather than out of any fundamental agreement with Nazi views of 'the Jews'.

A great deal of attention among historians has also focused on Italy's role in the origins of the Second World War. There is little doubt that Mussolini's invasion of Abyssinia greatly discredited the League of Nations. Mussolini's decision to abandon cordial relations with Britain and France in favour of closer relations with Nazi Germany also helped to strengthen Hitler's diplomatic position in the late 1930s. As a result, most historians accept that Mussolini was a key 'troublemaker' in the international relations of the 1930s. Even so, his foreign policy is not viewed by historians as pure aggression, but as being based on cold-blooded calculation of domestic factors, and was often guided by an awareness of the underlying military weakness of the Italian armed forces. It was these rational calculations which help to explain why Mussolini strove so energetically to prevent war in 1938 over Czechoslovakia, and why he did not go to war on Hitler's side in September 1939, even though he had signed a military alliance with the Nazi leader only a few months earlier. Even so, it is now accepted that Mussolini was always taking calculated risks in foreign policy, primarily to rally support for his regime inside Italy, which was constantly beset by economic problems. On the other hand, historians such as McGregor Knox suggest that Mussolini had a grand design for Italy to become a great European power. The only way to achieve this was to gamble all on Hitler winning the Second World War. This was a calculated risk which might have turned Italy into a major power, had Germany won the war. However, by entering into a close relationship with Hitler, Mussolini completely abandoned his earlier policy of leaving Italy with room for diplomatic manoeuvre, and this proved disastrous when Germany began to suffer a series of military defeats during the Second World War.

Summary questions

1 Identify and explain at least *two* factors which helped to destabilise Italy during the period 1918 to 1922.

2 Identify and explain the significance of at least *two* major domestic reforms in Italy under Mussolini.

3 Identify and explain at least *two* aspects of Mussolini's foreign and colonial policies during the inter-war period.

4 Identify and explain at least *two* factors which led to Mussolini's downfall during the Second World War.

6 Germany, 1918–45: the rise and fall of the Third Reich

Focus questions

◆ Why was the Weimar regime unstable?

◆ How did Hitler come to power in 1933?

◆ Did Hitler create an efficient system of government in Nazi Germany?

◆ What impact did the Nazis have on economic policy?

Significant dates

1919 *11 February* Ebert, a Social Democrat, becomes the first president of the Weimar Republic

1920 *March* An attempt to overthrow the democratic government, led by figures in the army (dubbed the 'Kapp putsch'), is foiled by a general strike

1921 *August* Erzberger, leader of the Catholic Centre Party, is assassinated by a right-wing extremist

1922 *June* Rathenau, the Jewish-born foreign minister and a key industrialist, is assassinated by an extreme right-wing faction

1923 *January* French and Belgian troops occupy the Ruhr
September The great inflation reaches its peak as the German currency collapses
November Munich beer hall putsch, led by Adolf Hitler, fails

1924 Dawes plan eases German reparation payments

1925 *February* President Ebert dies
April Hindenburg, former First World War military leader, is elected president
October Locarno treaties are signed

1929 *29 October* Wall Street crash in the USA triggers a world economic depression

1930 *March* Last democratic coalition, led by Müller, falls from power and is replaced by Brüning
September Hitler's Nazi Party gains 107 seats in Reichstag election

1932 *April* Hindenburg defeats Hitler in the presidential election by 19 million to 13 million votes
June Von Papen replaces Brüning as chancellor
July Nazi Party wins 230 seats at Reichstag election to become the most popular party in Germany

November Von Papen resigns
December General von Schleicher is appointed chancellor

1933 *30 January* Adolf Hitler replaces von Schleicher as chancellor, heading a coalition government
February Reichstag fire
March Hitler passes the Enabling Act, which gives him total dictatorial powers
June All political parties – except the Nazi Party – are dissolved

1934 *June* In the 'Night of the Long Knives', the Nazi leadership engages in a blood purge against 'socialist' elements within the Nazi Party and other political opponents
August Death of Hindenburg. Hitler assumes the role of president and adds the title of Führer. The army is obliged to swear an oath of allegiance to Hitler

1935 *September* Nuremberg laws strip Jews of civil and political rights

1936 *September* Four Year Plan to make Germany self-sufficient in food and raw materials is announced

1938 *November* *Kristallnacht* – a night of open violence against Jewish people – shocks the world

1939 *September* Outbreak of Second World War

1940 Victory for Nazi Germany in western Europe

1941 *June* Invasion of the Soviet Union by Nazi Germany

1943 *February* Defeat of German forces at Stalingrad by the Red Army is the major turning point of the Second World War

1944 *June* D-Day Landing by Britain and the USA opens up a second front in the European war

1945 *30 April* Hitler commits suicide
7 May Germany signs unconditional surrender, ending the Second World War and Nazi rule

Overview

The Weimar Republic (named after the town where its new constitution was agreed) was born in a period of national humiliation, economic chaos and civil disorder. The economic problems of Weimar Germany culminated in the 'great inflation' of 1923, which saw the savings of many Germans completely wiped out. The period between 1924 and 1929 brought a brief period of economic prosperity, but this was shattered by economic collapse in 1929, and was followed by high unemployment, and the increased use of emergency powers by the president. In this period Adolf Hitler's Nazi Party rose from relative obscurity to become the largest party in German politics. In January 1933, President Hindenburg appointed Hitler as chancellor in a coalition government, thus ending Germany's first experiment in democracy. The Nazi regime lasted from 1933 to 1945.

Why was the Weimar Republic unstable?

The Weimar Republic faced enormous difficulties from the very beginning. Germany had lost some 2 million troops in the war, and in the immediate post-war years the country suffered high unemployment, rampant inflation and bitter political differences between the right and left. A powerful myth, shared by many sections of German society, held that Germany had not been defeated in the First World War by the superior military power of its enemies, but was 'stabbed in the back' by socialist and democratic treachery at home. When the new Weimar government was forced by the Allies to sign the hated Versailles treaty, the stab-in-the-back myth seemed to be confirmed. From the very beginning, therefore, democratic government in Germany was like a candle awaiting a strong wind.

The constitution and the emergency powers of the president

The Weimar constitution contained many deep flaws. Germany remained a federal state, consisting of a central government with powers over finance and foreign affairs, and a series of regional governments, known as *Länder*, which enacted law at the local level. National power resided in the German parliament (Reichstag), located in Berlin, elected by all people over the age of 20. There was also a president, elected every seven years, who was given extensive emergency powers under article 48 of the constitution. The president was allowed to appoint and dismiss governments, and suspend civil rights, without parliamentary support, in a time of emergency. The first president, Friedrich Ebert, who ruled until 1925, used article 48 rarely, with the aim of sustaining democracy. The same was not true of **Paul von Hindenburg**, a leading army figure, and president from 1925 to 1934, who used article 48 frequently, in a manner which completely undermined the power of the Reichstag and democratic government.

The voting system

The voting system was based on proportional representation, and allocated seats in parliament on the basis of the overall number of votes cast for each party. This method, though fair, did encourage the growth of unstable **coalition governments**, and allowed all manner of small parties a voice in the Reichstag. In July 1932, for example, 27 different parties contested the election, and 15 gained seats. From 1919 to 1933, there were 21 different coalition governments, all of which contained no single dominant party. Most of these governments up to 1930 depended on the leading democratic parties:

1 the Social Democrats, the representatives of moderate labour;
2 the Catholic Centre Party, a religious-interest party;
3 the German People's Party, the representatives of industry.

Paul von Hindenburg (1847–1934) was a leading German general during the First World War. He advised the kaiser to abdicate in 1918. He was elected president of the Weimar Republic in 1925 and defeated Adolf Hitler comprehensively in the 1932 presidential election. He was responsible for the erosion of democracy in Germany from 1930 to 1933 by ruling through presidential decree under article 48 of the Weimar constitution. He was also responsible for inviting Hitler to become chancellor in January 1933. After his death in August 1934, Germany became a full-blown dictatorship.

A **coalition government** is one composed of two or more parties acting together to enact laws.

There were many other political parties whose members sat in the Reichstag, but which were completely opposed to democracy, including the Communist Party and the Independent Social Democrats, which both agitated for a Marxist revolution. On the extreme right there was a large number of nationalist and ultra-right-wing groups, including the Nazi Party, led by Adolf Hitler, which also desired the overthrow of the republic and its replacement by a military dictatorship.

Political instability and unrest

Political instability, with no party ever commanding an overall majority in the Reichstag, was a permanent feature of the fragile political life of the new republic. In January 1919, the Communist Party attempted an armed revolution in Berlin (the Spartacist revolt), which was defeated, against the odds, only with the help of the army and the paramilitary Freikorps, a group of ex-soldiers, who murdered two leading Communist leaders, Rosa Luxemburg and Karl Liebknecht. The Communist Party never forgave the Social Democrats for ordering the crushing of the Spartacist revolt. As a result, the left of German politics was bitterly divided.

Survival for the infant republic depended on the loyalty of the army, which prevented several attempts, from both the right and the left, to overthrow the government. In March 1920, for example, Dr Wolfgang Kapp led an army

A group of Freikorps troops, early in 1920.

coup (dubbed the 'Kapp **putsch**'), which aimed to set up a military dictatorship. In the early stages of the Kapp putsch, the leaders of the army refused to crush it. Only after a general strike, called by the trade unions, did the army decide to put the putsch down. Of the 775 army officers who had supported Kapp, however, only 48 lost their jobs.

A **putsch** is an illegal attempt to seize power.

Identify three reasons why the Weimar system was unstable.

Political violence

A constant feature of street life in Weimar Germany was political violence, which often bordered on civil war. Left- and right-wing paramilitary groups frequently engaged in pitched street battles, which often left several of the participants dead or seriously injured. Between 1918 and 1922, there were no less than 376 politically motivated murders. Many Communist Party leaders were assassinated in cold blood; and leading supporters of democracy, such as Matthias Erzberger, the leader of the Catholic Centre Party, and Walter Rathenau, a leading industrialist, were assassinated. In such a violent climate, the extreme parties of the right and left employed their own private paramilitary armies, and even the democratic parties ensured there were bouncers on the door of their meetings. The violence which surrounded politics simply added to the prevailing feeling of instability and gloom in German society.

The anti-democratic forces within the state

In such a deeply unstable political environment, the democratic government relied on the support of the judiciary, the civil service and the army to ensure its survival. Yet all these groups had very little sympathy with democracy. The judges of Weimar Germany, drawn from the upper classes, were anti-democratic in outlook and they punished the violence of the communist left much more harshly than crimes of right-wing groups. The civil service was also drawn from the upper echelons of German society, and used bureaucratic red tape to delay measures of social reform. The leading army officers, also from the old upper class, never really accepted Germany's military defeat in the First World War, had no empathy for democracy and longed for a return to the pre-1914 age of authoritarian and military rule. The army could be relied upon to crush left-wing revolt, but was reluctant to prevent right-wing violence.

The great inflation

Another fact of life in Weimar Germany was economic instability. Germany was in a state of severe economic recession in the years immediately following the First World War. From 1918 to 1923, the German mark fell, and inflation rose in a spectacular fashion. In 1920, the mark was worth 10 per cent of its 1914 value, but in January 1923 a single pre-1914 mark was worth 2,500 paper marks. In 1923, the price of a meal in a café could multiply 20 times between the time it took a diner to sit down at the table to eat it and go to the counter to pay for it.

The German government blamed the 'great inflation' on the demand by the Allies for reparations (see Chapter 4). Yet the German government, by printing vast quantities of paper money, and by allowing easy credit, was the architect of its own economic misfortune. In order to prevent a total economic collapse, a new currency, the rentenmark, based on land, was introduced and a national bank, designed to control the amount of printed money, was established. These measures helped to restore financial stability, especially in overseas financial markets.

Even so, the great inflation was a deeply traumatic experience for the German people, especially for the middle classes, who saw their pensions and life savings wiped out. There is little doubt that the middle classes had their confidence in democracy severely dented by this experience and their simmering resentment was later tapped effectively by Adolf Hitler's National Socialist Party in the midst of the economic depression from 1929 to 1933.

> In what ways did the great inflation damage the stability of the Weimar economy?

Economic miracle or mirage? The 'golden age of Weimar', 1924–29

In spite of the great inflation, the period 1924–29 witnessed a partial economic recovery in Germany. It gave some hope that Germany's miserable economic plight might be over. The economic upturn in Germany at this time was greatly helped by an $800 million loan from the USA under the Dawes plan (see page 87), which allowed Germany to re-equip its industry. From 1924 to 1929 wages rose above pre-war levels, and social and health schemes for workers added to the general sense of optimism. The inflow of foreign capital also helped local government to build new schools and hospitals.

Yet the extent of the economic recovery in Germany from 1924 to 1929 must not be exaggerated. Even in 1928, its peak year, unemployment stood at 1.8 million, and much of the improvement in the economy had been brought about through the constant injection of short-term foreign loans, especially from the USA. If this supply of short-term credit ceased, then Germany faced a complete economic collapse.

The Wall Street crash of 1929 and its consequences

In October 1929, the US stock market collapsed, setting in motion the most severe economic depression of the twentieth century. The most damaging effects of the Great Depression were felt in Germany. From 1924 to 1929, Germany had received $9 billion in US loans. As soon as these loans were no longer available, the German economy simply fell on its back. Unemployment rose from 1.8 million in 1928 to a staggering 6 million by 1932. Industrial production fell by 42 per cent and agricultural prices virtually collapsed, leaving many farmers bankrupt. The economic collapse which occurred after 1929 intensified feelings against the Weimar Republic, especially within middle-class communities, and among leading figures in business, agriculture and the army.

Briefly assess the significance of the Wall Street crash for the German economy.

The reparations problem

Foreign policy was another key source of political conflict in Weimar Germany. The battle between Germany and the Allies over the payment of reparations was the key issue of international affairs in the 1920s. The German people saw the payment of reparations as symbolic of everything they hated about the Versailles treaty. The whole issue came to a head when Germany defaulted on payments in November 1922. In January 1923, the French army, supported by the Belgians, occupied the Ruhr industrial region of Germany in a desperate attempt to make Germany pay. The German government supported a policy of passive resistance to the occupation.

The whole sorry episode showed that France, acting without British support, could not hope to force Germany to pay reparations. The German government realised a policy of continual non-payment was unlikely to produce any modification of the Versailles treaty. It was left to the USA to act as a mediator between Germany and the Allies. The outcome was the Dawes plan, under which Germany agreed to make regular annual reparation payments in return for a substantial US loan. At the same time, the French promised never to use force to gain payments in future, and ended the occupation of the Ruhr.

The influence of Stresemann

From 1924 to 1929, the German government took a conciliatory attitude towards the European powers. The key figure in this new policy of co-operation was Gustav Stresemann, the German foreign minister from 1924 to 1929, who had been chancellor for a brief period during 1923. The greatest symbol of Stresemann's conciliatory approach to foreign affairs was the signing of the Locarno treaties in 1925 by Germany, Britain, France and Italy. Under these agreements, Germany agreed to accept the western frontiers decided at Versailles, including the permanent demilitarisation of the Rhineland. In return, the Allies ended their military occupation of Cologne, and promised an early end to their military occupation of the Rhineland (this took place in 1930). In addition, the Allies ended military inspections of the German armed forces. Germany, in a further act of conciliation, agreed to join the League of Nations. Reparations were reduced further under the Young plan (1929) and were effectively ended at the Lausanne conference (1932).

Gustav Stresemann (1878–1929).

It seemed the Locarno treaties had laid the basis for a lasting solution to the 'German problem'. To most European diplomats, Germany, the 'spoiled child' of European diplomacy, seemed finally on a path of peace and reconciliation with the rest of Europe. However, this was an overoptimistic assessment. The German government had accepted its western frontiers under the Locarno treaties, but had made no such promise with regard to its eastern frontiers. In fact, Stresemann saw Locarno as the starting point for a complete revision of the Treaty of Versailles. Indeed, his foreign policy was double-edged. He was a peacemaker in public, while in private he held strong German nationalist views, with the long-term aim of recovering German territory in eastern Europe, albeit by peaceful negotiation, not military force.

The significance of Stresemann's death

The death of Stresemann on 3 October 1929 was a tragic blow for German foreign policy. No later German foreign minister combined such a conciliatory approach with such diplomatic skill. From 1930 to 1933, when Germany was ruled by presidential decree, German foreign policy was already moving away from peaceful collaboration with the Allies in order to revise Versailles, towards a more high-handed policy of 'going it alone' and engaging in unilateral action. In March 1931, for example, Brüning, the German chancellor, proposed a customs union with Austria. This caused a great outcry from the Allies, who were opposed to Germany joining with Austria in any manner, and was blocked by League of Nations pressure. In July 1932, moreover, Chancellor von Papen gave the go-ahead to the army for a secret programme of rearmament. It now seems clear that German foreign policy, after the death of Stresemann, and well before Hitler came to power, was already leading in the direction of attempting to revise the Treaty of Versailles by unilateral action.

> Suggest two reasons why Stresemann's death was a disaster for German foreign policy.

The collapse of democracy in Germany, 1930

In the same period as German foreign policy was starting to become more aggressive, the last truly democratic government of Weimar Germany – a fragile centre coalition, led by Hermann Müller and composed of the Social Democrats and members of both the German People's Party and the Catholic Centre Party – fell from power in March 1930. This was a grave moment in the history of Weimar democracy, because the Müller government was the last coalition which had a majority in the Reichstag. From March 1930 until January 1933, when Hitler came to power, Germany was governed by President Hindenburg, who used article 48 of the constitution to appoint a series of unstable cabinets with no majority in the Reichstag. Hindenburg, with the support of leading industrialists and army figures, effectively ended parliamentary government in 1930, a full three years before he finally called on Hitler to become German chancellor.

In March 1930, Hindenburg made Heinrich Brüning of the Catholic Centre Party chancellor in a so-called 'national government', which introduced a grim set of deflationary policies, including tax increases, pay reductions, redundancies and harsh cuts in public expenditure. This pushed the German economy further into recession. In a desperate attempt to give his regime some popular legitimacy, Brüning called a general election in September 1930. But the most startling feature of this election was the rapid growth of support for the Nazi Party, led by Adolf Hitler. The party increased its votes from 810,000 to 6.5 million and its seats in the Reichstag from 12 to 107, becoming the second largest party there, behind the Social Democrats. The arrival of Adolf Hitler on the centre-stage of German politics was to prove the final nail in the coffin of Weimar democracy.

> Explain briefly how Hindenburg undermined democracy in Germany before 1933.

How did Hitler come to power in 1933?

The rise of Adolf Hitler

Hitler was born on 20 April 1889 in Braunau am Inn, Austria. His father was a customs official, his mother a 'traditional housewife'. He was a failure at school, leaving at 16 without any qualifications. After the death of both his parents, he moved to Vienna in 1907 with the aim of becoming 'a great artist': quite a lofty ambition for a school failure. He stayed in Vienna from 1907 to 1913, attempting along the way to gain entry to the prestigious Academy of Arts. He was rejected on two occasions. Hitler then endured a brief period of unemployment, but eventually carved out a reasonable living as a commercial artist.

In 1913, Hitler fled across the Austrian–German border to Munich, to avoid being conscripted into the Austrian army. When the First World War began, he volunteered to join the German army (like many other Austrians, he identified with German nationalism and the idea of a pan-German union of German-speakers). He served with some distinction, gaining the Iron Cross, first class, for bravery, an honour very rarely given to a volunteer soldier. Hitler's period in the German army intensified his already extreme feelings of patriotism for the German cause. On the day news came of the German defeat in the war, Hitler was in hospital, recovering from a poison gas attack, and was utterly devastated. In July 1919, when Hitler heard the terms of the Treaty of Versailles, he decided to enter politics. His dream was to build a 'New Germany', under his own leadership, which would overturn the Treaty of Versailles and establish Germany as the major European power, en route to gaining revenge for the German defeat in the First World War.

In 1919, Hitler joined the German Workers' Party (DAP), a right-wing nationalist party, full of depressed ex-soldiers, under the leadership of Anton Drexler, a Munich locksmith. However, it soon became clear that Hitler was a very gifted speaker, with definite leadership qualities. In February 1920, the DAP became the National Socialist German Workers' Party (NSDAP, or Nazi Party, as it was commonly known), with Hitler soon emerging as its undisputed leader. The early programme of the Nazi Party called for a revision of Versailles and for democracy to be replaced by a military dictatorship.

In November 1923, Hitler led a coup (the Munich beer hall putsch), but this was a poorly planned attempt to seize power by force, which failed because of the loyalty of the German army and the local police force. Hitler stood trial for high treason, but served only 13 months in Landsberg Prison.

At this point, the career of Adolf Hitler, the rabble-rouser with a cause, seemed to be over. However, Hitler used his time in prison to define a new strategy for the Nazi Party, setting out his ideas in a book which he hoped would become a bible for his followers, and laying plans to give the Nazi Party a national organisation, which would be used to gain it power in democratic elections; that power would then be used to destroy democracy in Germany through a 'legal revolution'.

The book Hitler completed in Landsberg Prison was *Mein Kampf* (My struggle), a rambling part autobiography, part outline of his views on politics, and part diatribe on '**race**' and foreign affairs. Yet in *Mein Kampf*, Hitler laid out four key foreign policy aims, which were later carried out when he came to power:

1 the overturning of the Treaty of Versailles;
2 the gaining of territory (living space – **Lebensraum**) for Germany in eastern Europe through a war to defeat Soviet Bolshevism;
3 the inclusion of all German-speaking people in the Third Reich, especially in Austria, the Sudeten area of Czechoslovakia and the Danzig area given to Poland;
4 the creation of a racially pure German state, which would be the most dominant power in Europe.

The two new dimensions of Hitler's ideology were his desire to create a racially pure 'master race' of German people and his desire to see Jews 'eliminated' from all power and influence in Germany and throughout Europe.

The growth in support for the Nazi Party

From his release from prison in 1925 up to 1929, Adolf Hitler was a fairly well-known figure, leading a party which had made no significant breakthrough in democratic elections. In the German election of 1928, for example, the Nazi

Race is loosely used to define a group of people of common descent.

Lebensraum (living space) was the term used by Hitler to describe his aim of gaining territory for Germany in eastern Europe by military aggression.

Party gained only 2.6 per cent of the popular vote. Nazi electoral support was initially concentrated in small Protestant and rural towns in north-west Germany. It required something quite spectacular to transform the fortunes of the Nazi Party from a minor right-wing extreme party to a major party. Most historians believe it was the collapse of the German economy after 1929 which allowed Hitler to appeal successfully to members of the middle classes in towns and cities to vote for a party which seemed to promise a strong leader in charge of a patriotic government.

The growth of support for Adolf Hitler's Nazi Party requires some explanation. Its electoral share rose from 2.6 per cent of votes in 1928 to 37.3 per cent in 1932. The credit for this remarkable transformation must be given to Adolf Hitler's inspired leadership of the Nazis. After his release from prison, he changed from an impulsive and incompetent street fighter into a shrewd and skilful politician. He decided the road to power lay not through force alone, but by building a national movement, allied to successful propaganda. Under Hitler's leadership, the Nazi Party became a truly national party, which mobilised support in many areas which had previously had little interest in politics.

Nazi voting strength was higher in Protestant areas than in Catholic regions. The Nazis were never able to weaken support for the Catholic Centre Party, or the Bavarian People's Party, which also had the support of many Catholics. The major electoral advances for the Nazi Party from 1930 to 1932 were still mainly in rural Protestant areas, usually at the expense of the German National People's Party and the cluster of small right-wing special-interest parties which had emerged following the great inflation. The Nazis always attracted more new converts in regions where they did not face strong traditional religious or ideological loyalties to other parties.

The Nazi Party was more popular in small towns than in big cities and industrial regions. In the July 1932 election, for example, Nazi support in German cities with a population of over 100,000 was 10 per cent lower than in small towns. Members of the working class who voted Nazi came from small villages, with a population of less than 5,000. The hard core of Nazi support in the 1930 election was from the lower 'old' middle class in rural Protestant areas: shopkeepers, independent skilled workers and tradesmen, farmers and agricultural labourers. At the July 1932 election, however, the Nazis gained new support from the 'new' middle class: white-collar workers and upper-middle-class Protestants in the affluent suburbs, including teachers, doctors, civil servants and engineers. Many of these voters were hit by the depression and were attracted by the idea of a return to the 'golden days' before democracy had been introduced.

The majority of Nazi working-class support came from rural labourers and those in small-scale craft and domestic industries, in which workers were hostile to socialism and trade unions. The party failed to win substantial support from trade union members and industrial workers. More surprising, perhaps, is its complete failure to gain much support from the ranks of the unemployed, a group who featured prominently in Nazi propaganda. In those areas of Germany with the highest concentrations of unemployed industrial workers, the Communist Party, which was bitterly opposed to the Nazis – and democracy – enjoyed over 60 per cent of the vote.

Even so, the Nazi Party, the most anti-democratic of all the parties, did attract a much broader cross-section of public support than any other German political party. By July 1932, the Nazi Party was the largest party in the Reichstag. This was the high point of Hitler's electoral appeal. Even so, he was certainly nowhere near as popular as President Hindenburg, who gained 19.4 million votes, as opposed to the 13.4 million gained by Hitler at the 1932 presidential election. This illustrates the point that, under the proper rules of democracy, Hitler was by no means the all-powerful and popular figure which he appears to have been as the dictator of a one-party state. Indeed, at the November 1932 election, those parties which opposed the Nazi Party represented 63 per cent of the German electorate. In that same election, the Nazi Party lost 2 million votes, and had clearly passed the peak of its electoral popularity. Even so, the growth of the Nazi Party from complete obscurity in 1928 to becoming the largest party in the Reichstag in 1932 was a very significant factor in Hitler's rise to power, because it placed the Nazi leader in pole position to lead a right-wing authoritarian government, if that option was decided upon by Hindenburg. It was, therefore, those who voted for Hitler who helped to place him in a position to use his political skills to put pressure on Hindenburg to give him power.

> Identify the key groups from which the Nazi Party gained electoral support before 1933.

Hitler comes to power, 1933

In May 1932, Hindenburg sacked the deeply unpopular Brüning, and appointed Franz von Papen, an aristocratic member of the Catholic Centre Party, as chancellor in a government dubbed 'the cabinet of barons'. Von Papen immediately declared a state of emergency, suspended the Prussian regional parliament, the last stronghold of the Social Democrats, and called a general election in July 1932.

In the election, Hitler's Nazi Party gained 37.3 per cent of the votes, winning 230 seats, to become the largest party in the Reichstag. Hitler demanded to be made chancellor, but Hindenburg refused. The fall of von Papen, however, was not long delayed. In November 1932 he was driven out of office by a vote of no confidence in the Reichstag, passed by 512 votes to 46. By this stage, parliamentary government in Germany was tottering around like a punch-drunk boxer awaiting the inevitable knock-out blow.

DER MARSCHALL UND DER GEFREITE

MONTAGE BAUER MÜNCHEN

121

KÄMPFEN MIT UNS FÜR FRIEDEN UND GLEICHBERECHTIGUNG

A 1933 election poster, 'the marshal and the lance corporal': 'Fight with us for peace and equal rights'.

Hindenburg was coming under increasing pressure to appoint a government which had some popular support. A further election was held in November 1932, which saw the Nazi Party drop from 230 seats to 196, with a loss of almost 2 million votes. In December 1932, Hindenburg, still resisting Hitler's pleas to make him chancellor, decided to appoint a leading army figure, General von Schleicher, as chancellor. This move was designed to create a split within the Nazi Party, because von Schleicher believed Gregor Strasser, the most 'socialist'-minded Nazi, might be persuaded to join his coalition.

In January 1933, von Papen pressed Hindenburg to 'invite' Hitler to lead a coalition government. On 30 January, Hindenburg finally did so. While Hindenburg asked Hitler to form a 'national' coalition government, Hitler had the aim of establishing a right-wing authoritarian dictatorship, upholding the aims of the army, leading landowners and big business, with at least some semblance of popular support. Hitler came to power, therefore, with the agreement of Hindenburg, who hoped, or was at least persuaded, that Hitler could be harnessed to serve the needs of the old guard by leading a popular authoritarian government. The knock-out blow which ended Weimar democracy was therefore delivered by Hindenburg, not by Hitler.

Why was Hitler given power?

It is only against the background of the collapse of the Weimar political system that the decision to give Hitler power becomes clear. There was clearly a deep-seated crisis in the German political system, made worse by Hindenburg's dislike of democracy and his increasing use of arbitrary power under article 48.

There were also many people on the extreme right and the extreme left in German society who had no sympathy with democratic government. In the November 1932 election, for example, over 50 per cent of the votes went to the Nazi and Communist parties, which both wanted Germany to be a one-party state.

In January 1933, Hindenburg, having tried various right-wing alternatives, finally turned to Hitler as the last chance of establishing the strong authoritarian government, with some popular appeal, which he had been attempting to achieve ever since the fall of the last democratic government in 1930. It must be appreciated that Hindenburg and his supporters in the army, the aristocracy and industry were already in favour of using dictatorial and undemocratic methods to retain power.

Identify the key reasons why Hitler was brought to power in 1933.

By giving Hitler power, however, Hindenburg knew he was taking a risk. He did not, though, realise that Hitler would not be content to act as a puppet of the old authoritarian elite and the army. On the contrary, Hitler fully intended to create a state in which his own personal will would be dominant.

Historical interpretation: the rise of Hitler to power

The historical debate over the rise of Hitler has revolved around two key issues:

1 the vulnerability of Weimar democracy;
2 the strength and appeal of Hitler and the Nazi Party to the German people.

There are many historians who suggest that Hitler was brought to power by the authoritarian conservative right in the hope they could control him and use him to serve their ends. According to Alan Bullock, Hitler was 'jobbed into office by the old guard' at a time when his electoral popularity was 'on the wane'. Many other historians also suggest there was no 'inevitable' rise of Hitler to power. They argue the old conservative right could have found an alternative leader. According to this view, Hitler came to power in 1933 because of the weaknesses of a flawed democratic structure within Weimar Germany, which was dominated by reactionary forces on the right. In essence, these historians argue that the Weimar system was vulnerable to manipulation by the anti-democratic forces which controlled it. The democratic system in Germany from 1919 to 1933 was widely viewed by the conservative right as a 'stop-gap' form of government, which was 'unwanted and unloved'. It seems a great many Germans doubted whether democracy was superior to authoritarianism. Detlev Peukert has argued that Hitler's appeal to voters and to the conservative right who brought him to power lay in the fact that he promised a 'return to the past', using modern weapons. This appeal proved attractive to those groups within the right which desired a return to strong authoritarian government. As a result, Hitler turned the Nazi Party into the most popular party in Germany, not by stressing the radical anti-Semitic and anti-capitalist strands of the National Socialist programme, but by stressing that the party would take measures to weaken the power of socialism, and provide a strong government which would help the middle classes. As a result, most historians now view the destruction of democracy in Germany as being desired by a strong conservative power coalition, which brought Hitler into office to destroy the Weimar Republic and set up a conservative authoritarian regime – dominated by the old aristocracy, the army and big business. This proved a miscalculation, because Hitler intended to become an all-powerful dictator of his own Nazi regime, not the puppet of the old conservative and aristocratic German right.

Did Hitler create an efficient system of government in Nazi Germany?

Consolidation of power

Hitler came to power in January 1933 with the full backing of the traditional ruling elite, the army, big business and most German middle-class voters. Yet there were still many formidable obstacles in his path to establishing a Nazi dictatorship. Only three Nazis – Hitler, Wilhelm Frick, the minister of the interior, and Hermann Göring, minister without portfolio, were included in the coalition government. Hitler did not even have a majority in the Reichstag. Nor could he rely on the full support of the army in all circumstances. Big business gave Hitler support only on the understanding that he would not threaten large private companies. What is more, the president, under article 48, retained the power to dismiss him.

In spite of these barriers, Hitler moved very quickly and decisively during 1933 to consolidate his hold on power. This was greatly aided by two laws, passed shortly after he became German chancellor. The first was a decree, issued on 28 February 1933, for the 'protection of the people and state'. This wide-ranging set of emergency measures allowed Hitler to suspend all civil liberties, assume control of state government and put all political opponents in 'protective custody'. It was originally announced as a temporary measure (enacted the day after the Reichstag had been burnt down in a fire, started by a crazed Dutch communist, Marinus van der Lubbe), but this 'state of emergency' was to remain in force during the entire Nazi period of rule.

The second key law used by Hitler to increase his dictatorial hold over Germany was the Enabling Act. This was made law shortly after the Nazis held the last democratic election in Germany, the only one under Hitler's rule, in March 1933. The Act (entitled the Law for the Alleviation of the Distress of People and Reich) was passed by 441 to 84 votes in the Reichstag on 23 March 1933, with only the brave Social Democrats voting against. It was extremely important in the establishment of a dictatorship in Germany because it allowed Hitler to pass laws without any restraint from the Reichstag or the president.

The revolution after power

Hitler used these two emergency laws to enact a 'legal revolution' in Germany during 1933. The process towards Nazi dominance over the nation was called co-ordination (*Gleichschaltung*). Local government was brought under the control of Nazi-appointed governors (*Gauleiter*), and regional parliaments were quickly abolished. By the summer of 1933, trade unions and all political parties, except the Nazi Party, had been dissolved. The free press was brought swiftly under Nazi direction. The Nazis took control of the police, and political opponents were arrested and confined to concentration camps. By the end of 1933, Hitler was the head of a one-party state. This revolution had used the legal power of the German state to destroy democracy. However, the power of the president, the army and big business remained largely untouched. The army was happy to watch the destruction of democracy because Hitler promised vast rearmament. Big business greatly welcomed the abolition of strikes and trade unions and was reassured by Hitler's promise not to interfere with private enterprise.

However, within the Nazi Party there was a group of radicals with strong anti-capitalist views, who started calling for a 'second Nazi revolution'. This was designed – in the minds of the Nazi radicals – to weaken the power of the army and big business within the German state. Most Nazi radicals were clustered around Ernst Röhm, the hard-nosed leader of the Storm Troopers (SA), the grass-roots street fighters of the movement. Röhm's most controversial idea was to turn the existing German army into a people's army led by the SA and the SS (*Schutzstaffel*) – Hitler's personal bodyguard. Not surprisingly, the

Ernst Röhm, leader of the SA (in the centre of the picture), with Göring on his left. Hitler is giving the Nazi salute. Röhm was murdered a year later on the Night of the Long Knives. His successor, Lutze, is standing to his right.

call of the SA for a 'second revolution' made the army and members of big business very anxious indeed.

Matters came to a head during the summer of 1934, when President Hindenburg, supported by the army leadership, put pressure on Hitler to purge the SA or face the prospect of losing power altogether. Hitler, who had little sympathy with the anti-capitalist ideas of the radicals, did fear the army might topple him from power. As a result, he decided (with some reluctance) to crush the SA, primarily because he required the support of the army to stay in power, and he needed its officers to carry out his foreign policy objectives. Without doubt, the army was the one traditional conservative force which Hitler truly feared during the early years of his dictatorship.

On 30 June 1934, Hitler, supported by the SS, engaged in a brutal and lawless night of killing – the 'Night of the Long Knives' – mostly of the leaders of the SA, but also of many other Nazi radicals and other political opponents. It seems about 400 old enemies of Hitler were killed during this night of state-sponsored murder, including Röhm, Strasser, the Nazi radical, and General von Schleicher, the former German chancellor. Hindenburg and the army leadership thought the blood purge was necessary for the 'defence of the state'.

This event greatly consolidated Hitler's dictatorship. On 2 August 1934, President Paul von Hindenburg died. Hitler swiftly announced he would

Führer is the German word for 'leader'.

become president and **Führer** of the German nation. Hitler also used Hindenburg's death to force the army to swear an oath of personal allegiance to him as commander of the armed forces and head of state. The army, grateful that Hitler had already destroyed the SA, did not object to this. Indeed, from 1934 to 1938, the army leadership still thought of itself as an equal partner with Hitler over the German nation. This confidence within the old officer class of the army was somewhat misplaced. The power of the army to make its own decisions was being gradually eroded by Hitler. The swastika was placed on army uniforms. Officers had to accept Nazi instruction from SS officers before qualification. What the army leadership did not fully appreciate was that the purge of the SA in 1934 had been desired by the SS, led by Heinrich Himmler, which now became a fierce rival to the army and a dominant influence over Hitler within the Nazi state. After 1936, Hitler time and time again forced the army to follow his own decisions on foreign policy, often against the generals' own better judgement. In February 1938, Hitler took complete control over the whole of the armed forces.

Briefly outline the key events in Hitler's consolidation of power.

The Nazi state

The Nazi state was led by one dominant leader (Adolf Hitler), who was also the leader of the only legal political party in Germany (the Nazi Party). Yet Nazi Germany, although it is often called a one-party state, was actually a personal dictatorship, dominated by Hitler, who had seemingly unlimited power over the German people, and who was supported by a number of powerful groups: the army, big business, the Nazi Party and the SS–Gestapo.

Heinrich Himmler (1900–45).

However, Hitler could not control every decision. As a result, decision-making was undertaken by a Nazi elite and a number of state and Nazi organisations. Hitler greatly disliked administration and he left most decisions on domestic issues to ministers. He very rarely called cabinet meetings and he dealt with each minister separately. The major requirement for a law to be passed in Nazi Germany was the signature of Adolf Hitler. Hitler often undermined the power of his individual cabinet ministers by setting up rival organisations. It has been estimated that 42 different agencies were given power by Hitler to enact different aspects of policy. He was aware that the government structure of Nazi Germany was very poorly co-ordinated, but he constantly blocked moves to create a centralised structure.

Disagreements among the ruling elite in the Nazi state were not about Hitler's power, which was supreme, but revolved around which Nazi minister was most loyally carrying out the 'Führer's will', which, of course, was open to wide interpretation. Ministers fought long-running feuds with each other, which served to cause divisions and made it difficult for decisions from above to be carried out effectively at grass-roots level.

One of the key reasons for the administrative chaos in the Nazi state was Hitler's refusal to create a new constitution, to help define the role of the Nazi Party. Hitler never made it clear whether the Nazi Party was superior or subordinate to the decisions of state officials at national or regional level. It is now generally agreed among historians that Nazi Germany was far less orderly and efficient than was generally supposed. Indeed, Hitler is now viewed as administratively incompetent, allowing German government to degenerate at national and local level into chaos and anarchy.

Suggest two reasons why Nazi Germany was not administratively efficient.

What impact did the Nazis have on economic policy?

The economy

Adolf Hitler had little direct interest in economic policy. The political platform of the Nazi Party had been built on promises to abolish large department stores, curb big business and give help to small traders, shopkeepers and farmers. However, Hitler proved very lukewarm to the anti-big-business aspects of the Nazi programme once in power. It is pretty clear that Hitler was not opposed to big business or capitalist free enterprise. He wanted German businessmen to prosper, and for the German economy to become self-sufficient.

The most important figure in Nazi economic policy from 1933 to 1937 was Dr Hjalmar Schacht, a leading Conservative banker, who was not even a member of the Nazi Party. The most important economic policy Schacht followed was the 'New Plan', introduced in 1934. It froze all interest on foreign debts, and was underpinned by a series of bilateral trade agreements with foreign countries, which aided German exports and ensured cheap imports from eastern Europe and South America. Schacht also created an ingenious system of internal credit which enabled rapid rearmament to be financed by printing money.

Hjalmar Schacht (1877–1970), the German economist who masterminded Nazi Germany's apparent economic recovery.

The most impressive aspect of Nazi economic policy in peacetime was the sharp fall which took place in unemployment – from 5 million in 1932 to less than 1 million in 1937. This was described at the time as an 'economic miracle'. But it was largely achieved by state-aided, low-pay, job-creation schemes on public works programmes, the introduction of conscription – which ended youth unemployment – and new jobs in the expanding armaments industry. It is now generally agreed by economic historians that the Nazi regime created artificial jobs, which would only have brought about inflation, and possible economic collapse, had Germany not started the Second World War.

The only major intervention by Hitler in the field of economic policy was the Four Year Plan, introduced in September 1936, under the leadership of Göring. The Four Year Plan (the title copied from Stalin's 'Five Year Plans') aimed to make Germany self-sufficient in food and raw materials in preparation for war. Under the plan, imports were to be reduced and industries that produced synthetic alternatives to imported raw materials were offered vast state subsidies. In addition, farmers were offered incentive payments to produce more food. However, the Four Year Plan was a failure. In 1939, Germany was still importing 20 per cent of its food and 33 per cent of its raw materials. The German economy was not close to collapse in 1939, but the need for injections of cash and raw materials through short wars or occupations had become very important. The German economy was never fully prepared for a lengthy war. Indeed, it was only in 1943, when Germany started suffering military defeats, that the economy was brought under central control, but this was too late to prevent the German defeat by the Allies in May 1945.

> Outline the key economic policies followed by the Nazi regime in the 1930s.

Historical interpretation: Nazi Germany

The historical debate over Nazi Germany has generated enormous controversy. The most dominant figure in all historical studies of Nazi Germany is Adolf Hitler. A great deal of attention has focused recently on the myth and the reality of Hitler's power within Nazi Germany. On the one hand are the 'intentionalist' group of historians, who claim Hitler was the 'complete master' of the Third Reich; on the other are the 'structuralist/functionalist' historians, who emphasise Hitler's ignorance of administrative matters and show him to have been a rather 'weak dictator' who was never fully in control of the government machine.

Ian Kershaw has recently suggested that a distinction should be drawn between the powerful myth, created by Nazi propaganda, of Hitler as an efficient and all-powerful dictator and the reality of the Nazi state, which was a positive minefield of conflicting spheres of authority. It has been shown that individual Nazi ministers and agencies were allowed a wide degree of flexibility in how policies were implemented. In response, the intentionalists have argued that the chaos in Nazi government was a deliberate ploy by Hitler to divide and rule over his subordinates on domestic policy in order to retain a dominant position over the key issues which mattered to him, which lay in the areas of foreign policy and military matters.

Another key area of debate among historians concentrates on whether Nazi rule produced a social revolution in German society. There are historians who believe that the Nazi regime did break the stranglehold of traditional German conservative elites, and helped to introduce a less hierarchical, more classless society. However, most historians are sceptical about the argument of a social revolution in Nazi Germany. Some have suggested Nazi rule strengthened class differences and favoured big business and the military, while depriving the working class of free trade unions, free speech and employment rights. The civil service, the army officer group, the judiciary and universities went on recruiting from the same upper-class groups from which they always had. Even the SS – usually viewed as the most important Nazi organisation within the state – was increasingly drawn after 1933 from the old landowning upper classes. To those historians who have examined everyday life in Nazi Germany, the idea of a social revolution is even less convincing. Detlev Peukert showed that Nazi Germany was very little different in its class structure, and its distribution of power and wealth, from the democratic capitalist societies, such as Britain, France and the USA. The Nazi 'social revolution' is now viewed as one of the major propaganda myths surrounding the regime.

Most historians also agree that the Nazi regime did not produce any distinctive economic policies. Hitler did not weaken the power or position of wealthy private businessmen or major German companies. The Nazi policy of using government money to put people in jobs was favoured, even in the 1930s, by the British economist John Maynard Keynes, and formed part of President Roosevelt's New Deal in the USA. Even the drive for self-sufficiency was borrowed from Stalin's idea of 'socialism in one country'. Yet the Four Year Plan was a complete failure. Indeed, most historians now agree that Nazi Germany provided an economic climate which greatly aided the profits of private enterprise and giant monopoly companies. The destruction of trade unions and the employment rights of workers, and the adoption of slave labour, all served to increase the power of large companies over their workers, and their profits. If Germany had won the war, German companies could have continued to use slave labour to increase profits. It is now becoming accepted by historians that Nazi Germany was a power coalition in which a Nazi elite grew wealthy, the army remained powerful, and big business increased profits and exploited labour.

Increasingly, historians are exposing many of the propaganda myths surrounding the regime, to reveal the reality of life inside Nazi Germany. Hitler is increasingly being placed within a political context that would scarcely have seemed possible over 30 years ago. It is now accepted by most historians that Hitler's rule in Nazi Germany was less **totalitarian** than that in Stalin's Russia or Mao's China. In peacetime, it was also less brutal than either of those regimes. It is even doubtful whether Hitler can be viewed as the most evil dictator of the twentieth century. The idea of Nazi Germany as an efficient state which created a social revolution is even less plausible.

Totalitarian is used to describe a government which permits no rival political parties and attempts to gain total control over society.

It now seems clear that Hitler had no clear control over what was really happening in Nazi Germany and allowed administrative chaos to become part of the government machine. These revelations about the nature of Hitler's rule help to explain why the Nazi regime went on to suffer such a catastrophic defeat when it was faced with a coalition of more formidable rivals during the Second World War. Indeed, we must remember that Weimar Germany's experiment with democracy, for all its supposed faults, actually lasted over two years longer than Hitler's experiment with dictatorship in Germany.

Summary questions

1 Identify any *two* factors which made the Weimar Republic unstable in the early 1920s.

2 Compare the importance of at least *three* reasons for Hitler's rise to power in Germany.

3 Identify and explain any *two* factors which contributed to the popularity of the Nazis in the 1930s.

4 Identify and explain any *two* factors which helped to increase Hitler's power in Germany after 1933.

7

The origins of the Second World War

Focus questions

◆ What impact did the First World War have on the origins of the Second World War?

◆ What role did the Great Depression play in destabilising international affairs?

◆ How important was ideology in the conflict between nations during the 1930s?

◆ Was Hitler primarily to blame for the outbreak of the Second World War?

◆ What part did the policy of appeasement play in the origins of the Second World War?

Significant dates

1933	*January*	Hitler comes to power in Germany
	October	Germany leaves the League of Nations
1934	*January*	Germany signs non-aggression pact with Poland
1935	*March*	Hitler announces German rearmament
	April	Stresa Front, signed by Britain, France and Italy, pledges to halt unilateral breaches of international treaties
	June	Anglo-German naval agreement is signed
1935	*October*	Italy invades Abyssinia
1936	*March*	German troops march into the Rhineland
	July	Spanish Civil War breaks out
	October	Rome–Berlin Axis is signed
1937	*May*	Neville Chamberlain, pledged to follow a 'policy of appeasement' towards Germany and Italy, becomes British prime minister
1938	*March*	Germany occupies Austria
	September	Munich agreement ratifies German take-over of the Sudetenland area of Czechoslovakia
1939	*March*	Germany occupies Czechoslovakia
	May	Pact of Steel is signed between Germany and Italy
	August	Nazi–Soviet pact is signed
	1 September	Germany invades Poland
	3 September	Britain and France declare war on Germany

Overview

On 3 September 1939, Britain and France declared war on Germany. Ever since, the causes of the Second World War have been the subject of endless debate. The war came as a result of a military attack by Nazi Germany on Poland on 1 September 1939, but this was part of a build-up of tension in European relations during the 1930s. It is possible to view the outbreak of war by reference to short-term events in 1939, but the idea that such a momentous conflict was due to a short-term crisis ignores the deep-seated problems out of which the war emerged.

In discussing the origins of the Second World War, we must look at long-term causes, which are often called origins. It is these long-term factors which help to create the disputes and conflicts which later create a crisis which develops into war. They provide the background to the short-term causes, in particular the major events which were decisive in the actual outbreak of war. We must also examine the key leaders who took the decisions to go to war and evaluate their policies.

What impact did the First World War have on the origins of the Second World War?

One of the most important long-term factors in the outbreak of the Second World War was the impact of the First World War. The war left a legacy of economic problems, most notably a collapse of world trade, high unemployment, agricultural depression, war debts, unstable currencies and hyper-inflation. Few people wanted a repetition of a conflict which had killed so many people. As a result, there was great disenchantment with the use of force in international relations. This public mood greatly influenced the peacemakers who met in Paris in 1919 with the intention of creating a settlement which would help to prevent war in future.

The Paris peace settlement and its consequences

The Paris peace settlement of 1919 has been viewed as a major cause of the Second World War. It has been claimed that the peace settlement failed to solve the problems which had caused the First World War and created new problems which encouraged the outbreak of a second major conflict. Of course, we can now see the magnitude of the task facing the peacemakers. The leaders of the countries which drafted the peace settlement – Britain, France, the USA and Italy – did want to prevent a future war, not bring one about. Even so, major errors were made. Within 20 years, Europe was back at war.

The Treaty of Versailles

The Treaty of Versailles has been singled out as the most glaring failure of the peace settlement. The peacemakers viewed German militarism as the chief cause of the war, and they decided a number of precautions were needed to prevent a German military revival. The Germans considered the Versailles treaty as very unjust. Of course, we can now see that they were being completely unrealistic in expecting a more lenient settlement. It seems the German people expected a peace treaty which punished them very little. Perhaps the real problem with the Treaty of Versailles was not its harshness but its underlying leniency. It did not rule out a German military revival. Indeed, the creation of a number of small and weak independent powers in eastern Europe left Germany in a very good position to dominate that region once again, if it could shake off the military restrictions imposed at Versailles.

The League of Nations

The second key failure of the 1919 peace settlement was the League of Nations. The idea was for the League to act as an arbitrator in disputes between nations, and to provide collective security in the event of military aggression. The League, on paper at least, had the power to impose economic sanctions and, if they failed, to threaten an aggressor with collective military action by all its members. It seemed a good idea at the time. The burden of keeping the peace was to be shared by all nations. It was believed the League would end the selfish diplomacy of nation-states. But these ideas were completely untested in the hard-faced world of international relations. The League could work effectively only if it had the support of all the world's great powers. But the USA was not a member – and when the League was called upon to deal with military aggression during the 1930s it proved completely ineffective.

In 1931, Japan invaded Manchuria, but the League failed to act. It took no action when Italy invaded Abyssinia in 1935. It also proved unable to prevent Germany from rearming, and did not prevent the Spanish Civil War, which broke out in 1936. By 1938, the League of Nations had ceased to be an effective international peacekeeper. It was to play no significant role in the key events which led to war. The collapse of the League left international relations in a state of confusion in the late 1930s, a confusion which Hitler exploited.

Identify two major weaknesses of the League of Nations.

What role did the Great Depression play in destabilising international affairs?

The role of the Great Depression in encouraging international instability must be considered when evaluating the causes of the Second World War. It was triggered by the collapse of the Wall Street stock market in October 1929. It was followed by the most prolonged economic depression of the twentieth century. The most damaging consequences of the depression were felt in Germany. It was in the midst of the depression that Adolf Hitler's Nazi Party rose to become the largest party in Germany, which greatly aided Hitler's accession to office in 1933.

It is very important to recognise the significance of the Great Depression on the unstable international relations of the 1930s. The optimism for peace in the 1920s gave way to the self-preservation of the 'hungry' 1930s. The depression plunged the free market into a major crisis. Most countries adopted protectionism and turned inwards to deal with social and economic problems. Democratic government was also challenged by new dynamic totalitarian regimes, with state-run economies, ruled by charismatic dictators such as Stalin, Hitler, Mussolini and Franco. In comparison, democratic leaders looked dull and ineffective.

How important was ideology in the conflict between nations during the 1930s?

Ideology was another important ingredient in the causes of the Second World War. It is very tempting to view the 1930s as a period of intense ideological conflict which eventually produced a military conflict. The inter-war period saw the emergence of three very different ideologies.

1 Germany, Italy and Japan had regimes which expressed extreme nationalist ideologies that supported military aggression and increased arms spending.
2 The Soviet Union (modern-day Russia) was led by supporters of Marxist-Leninist ideas, who had spoken of the need for a world-wide revolution of the workers.
3 Britain, France and the USA had democratic regimes and free elections – and foreign policies which favoured peace.

These deep ideological differences made international co-operation very difficult. Each power was often pulling in a different direction. If a key cause of war is a breakdown of diplomacy, then the differing ideologies of the great powers during the 1930s clearly made a major contribution to the outbreak of the war.

The real question in assessing the role of ideology is deciding which ideology was the most disruptive to international harmony. The real troublemakers – or warmongers – in Europe were Germany and Italy, and in the Far East Japan, which also had a nationalist regime. Yet, as we have already seen, Mussolini's foreign policy was not pure aggression, but was based on cold-blooded calculations of national self-interest. Mussolini was a disruptive force in the

Hitler at a mass rally in Nuremberg demonstrating the military might of Nazi Germany.

mid-1930s, especially in ordering the invasion of Abyssinia, which greatly undermined the League of Nations, but Mussolini played a conciliatory role during the Czech crisis of 1938, and in September 1939 he did not go to war alongside Nazi Germany, even though he had a military pact with Hitler.

The chief troublemaker in Europe was unquestionably Adolf Hitler and his Nazi ideology. Nazism was projected as the will of a single individual in charge of a strong military state. It is difficult to understand why Hitler was spending so much money on armaments when he had no need to, unless war was a key aim of his foreign policy.

> Briefly outline the major features of the competing ideologies in Europe in the inter-war period.

Was Hitler primarily to blame for the outbreak of the Second World War?

The chief cause of the Second World War was, therefore, the foreign policy objectives of Adolf Hitler. Hitler was determined to ensure that the peace settlement of 1919 collapsed. Indeed, if the politicians in Britain and France had been as determined to uphold the peace settlement as strongly as Hitler was determined to destroy it, then there may never have been a Second World War. Unless Hitler was prepared to halt German expansion voluntarily – and to enter into some new negotiated settlement of German grievances – then war was fairly certain to break out at some point in the late 1930s.

Indeed, the Second World War might have happened much earlier than September 1939 as Hitler moved step by step to overturn the peace settlement of 1919. He withdrew Germany from the League of Nations in 1933, announced German rearmament in 1935, sent German troops into the Rhineland in 1936,

Map 3. The territorial expansion of Nazi Germany, 1936–39.

brought Austria into Germany in 1938, threatened war over Czechoslovakia in 1938 and – though he signed the Munich agreement in the same year – occupied that country in March 1939.

What Hitler did by these actions was to build up tension in Europe to boiling point. His opponents were constantly being faced with a stark choice – capitulate to Hitler's demands or fight a war to stop him. In March 1939, when Hitler occupied Czechoslovakia, it was clear his actions were certainly leading in the direction of dominating Europe by force. The only question left when Hitler threatened Poland in 1939 was not what would Hitler do but what would Britain and France do to stop him. In September 1939, Poland decided to fight, and Britain and France declared war. Force became the only option left because Hitler would not negotiate on equal terms with any other power.

Hence, in order to explain why war ultimately broke out in September 1939, the role of Hitler is crucial. There is abundant evidence to show that all the major decisions on foreign policy in Germany were taken by Hitler and this makes his aims vitally important. These aims, as outlined in *Mein Kampf*, do represent a blueprint for action. The key aims of Hitler's foreign policy were:

1 to destroy the Treaty of Versailles;
2 to include all German-speakers in the Third Reich, especially those in Austria and Czechoslovakia;
3 to gain territory (*Lebensraum*, or living space) in eastern Europe at the expense of the Soviet Union;
4 to make Germany the most dominant power in Europe – a sort of superpower – and then probably make a bid for world domination.

It would be unwise – as A. J. P. Taylor once did – to dismiss Hitler's aims as 'coffee house dreaming'. On the contrary, they do amount to a framework for action, pursued as a set of objectives to be achieved stage by stage. When Hitler did compromise or improvise his aims – for example by signing the Munich agreement in 1938 or by signing the Nazi–Soviet pact with Stalin (his sworn ideological enemy) in 1939 – he did so for a tactical reason, and in both these cases he did not abandon his ultimate objectives, but rather only postponed them.

> Evaluate briefly Hitler's role in the outbreak of the Second World War.

What part did the policy of appeasement play in the origins of the Second World War?

However, alongside the view that Hitler was the chief culprit in the outbreak of the Second World War lies a second explanation, which puts a great deal of the blame for the outbreak of war not exclusively on Hitler but also on **Neville Chamberlain** and the policy of **appeasement**. As Winston Churchill said in 1946, 'There was never a war in all history easier to prevent by timely action than the one which has just desolated great areas of the globe. It could have been prevented without firing a shot, but no one would listen.'

The aim of the policy of appeasement was to satisfy the grievances left behind by the Paris peace settlement in the hope that these concessions, brought about by negotiation, would satisfy Hitler and encourage him to live in peace and harmony with the rest of Europe. The most famous supporter of this policy was Neville Chamberlain, the British prime minister from 1937 to 1940, but the policy was also followed by the French government in the run-up to the war.

Of course, it is easy to blame Chamberlain and to see him as a selfish and deluded politician, but we must remember that successive British and French

Neville Chamberlain (1869–1940) was British prime minister from 1937 to 1940. Although he was a very successful chancellor of the exchequer from 1931 to 1937, who helped to guide Britain out of the depression, his reputation has always been tarnished by his association with the policy of appeasing Hitler, which failed to prevent the outbreak of the Second World War. In recent times, Chamberlain's poor reputation has been revived somewhat by a number of revisionist historians who have suggested that, far from being taken in by Hitler, Chamberlain 'hoped for the best' but 'prepared for the worst' by sanctioning the building of the fighter aircraft which enabled Britain to prevent a Nazi invasion during the Battle of Britain. On the other hand, the policy of appeasement is still viewed (especially by the USA – the most dominant military power) as not the best means of dealing with an obvious aggressor. Chamberlain died of cancer in 1940 during the period when Britain stood alone against Nazi Germany.

Appeasement is a diplomatic policy which aims to settle grievances of nations by negotiation rather than military force. Appeasement is most closely associated with Neville Chamberlain's mission to pacify German grievances from 1937 to 1939. Ever since it has been defined as a policy stance taken from a position of military weakness when faced with a likely or obviously aggressive power.

"EUROPE CAN LOOK FORWARD TO A CHRISTMAS OF PEACE", SAYS HITLER

A David Low cartoon highlighting the outcome for Europe of the policy of appeasement.

governments from 1933 had done little to halt the march of aggression, nor taken steps to strengthen the power of the League of Nations. We can say the same thing about the USA, which followed a policy of isolationism in the 1930s.

By 1937, when Chamberlain came to power, the USA, Germany, Italy and Japan had all left the League of Nations, and Chamberlain felt the organisation had no further role to play. There is little doubt that Chamberlain's personality – he was self-confident, obstinate and stubborn – did play a crucial part in the events which led to war. Chamberlain decided that the only way to sustain long-term peace was to get Germany, Italy and Japan to take part in a new general settlement of all outstanding issues – to be agreed and accepted by all sides.

But what Chamberlain did not want – and could not offer – was a free hand for Hitler to dominate central and eastern Europe. Yet these were the only terms that Hitler was willing to accept. Hence, the differing aims of Hitler and Chamberlain meant that the policy of appeasement was doomed to failure from the start, which must lead us to discuss why it was pursued for so long. Any consideration of appeasement must mention several factors.

1 There was a widespread horror of war in Britain and France.

2 Too much faith had been placed in the League of Nations.

3 There was a great deal of sympathy in Britain with the idea that Germany had been punished too harshly by the Treaty of Versailles, and the policy of appeasement was sympathetic to Hitler's desire to revise the treaty.

4 British public opinion constantly opposed rearmament.

5 The poor state of Britain's armed forces also encouraged the policy of appeasement.

6 The French had no real stomach for another war with Germany.

7 There was an ideological dislike of the Soviet Union, which meant that Chamberlain preferred doing business with Hitler to entering an alliance with Stalin.

It was an intermingling of all these factors which made Chamberlain follow appeasement, but it must be appreciated that Chamberlain pursued the policy almost like a religious fanatic. He would not contemplate any other.

Indeed, Chamberlain's attempts to find an alternative policy to appeasement after March 1939, when Hitler occupied Czechoslovakia, showed a distinct lack of judgement. He chose to offer a guarantee to Poland – a country Britain could not defend. Even more disastrous, he delayed signing an alliance with the Soviet Union in the summer of 1939, a delay which allowed Hitler to offer Stalin a pact which kept the Soviet Union out of the war in September 1939 and left the decision for war in the hands of the Polish government. Hence, the failed policy of appeasement served to illustrate the weakness of British and French resolve to resist Hitler, and was accompanied by errors of judgement which played a crucial role in the outbreak of the Second World War. Oddly enough, it was Chamberlain who declared war on Germany – not Hitler who declared war on Britain.

Neville Chamberlain (1869–1940).

Identify the chief reasons why Chamberlain adopted a policy of appeasement.

Historical interpretation: the origins of the Second World War

The dominant interpretation of the origins of the Second World War was originally advanced by Hugh Trevor Roper, and supported by Alan Bullock. This holds that Hitler's views as outlined in *Mein Kampf*, which aimed to make Germany a major European power by gaining *Lebensraum* in eastern Europe by military force, were a blueprint for his foreign policy actions in power and led to an escalating crisis in the 1930s which eventually brought about the outbreak of the Second World War. This interpretation, although challenged by A. J. P. Taylor, who claimed that Hitler did not want a major European war to break out in 1939, remains the most dominant explanation.

Even so, the role of Neville Chamberlain and the policy of appeasement have come under scrutiny. Appeasement has been viewed as a 'diplomacy of illusion', which failed to appreciate that Hitler wanted to dominate Europe by force and was unappeasable. It has also been argued that a second fatal 'illusion' of Chamberlain was to negotiate with the Nazi dictator from a position of military weakness. As a result, appeasement is viewed by many historians as presenting Hitler with easy opportunities to advance German territorial aims in Europe, without providing Britain or France with any insurance against the possibility of further aggression. In more recent times, some 'revisionist' historians have sought to show the economic and military weaknesses which helped to guide Chamberlain's policy, but they have never proved that appeasement was a sensible policy to deal with the specific problems of Hitler's dynamic foreign policy. Indeed, a new group of 'post-revisionist' historians now argue that Chamberlain's strength of will helped to demolish alternative policies, which may have stopped Hitler, such as a military alliance between Britain, France and Russia. They also argue that Chamberlain encouraged Hitler to believe, when he attacked Poland in September 1939, that his 'spineless opponents' in Britain and France would not go to war to stop his military aggression. In essence, therefore, the Second World War broke out because of the dynamic foreign policy of Hitler and the diplomatic mistakes and weaknesses of his opponents.

Document study
Nazi Germany, 1933–45

Focus questions

◆ How effectively did Hitler establish and consolidate Nazi authority?

◆ What was the impact of Nazi policies on German society?

◆ How did the Nazis deal with the 'Jewish question'?

◆ What impact did Nazi economic policies have on Germany in the 1930s?

◆ What was the impact of the war on the popularity of Hitler and the Nazi regime?

◆ What was the nature of the resistance to the Nazi regime?

Overview

Attempting to evaluate the impact of Nazi rule or Hitler's popularity on German society is extremely difficult. After all, Nazi Germany was a dictatorship. Nazi propaganda claimed that Hitler was determined to create a *Volksgemeinschaft*, a people's community, which would end old class divisions and create a truly classless society based on merit, not privilege. Yet Hitler had no thoroughly worked-out social or economic policies. It is now widely accepted by historians that the Nazi regime was primarily concerned with moulding the attitudes of the German people towards offering support for Hitler's policies.

By the end of 1934, Hitler had swept away all the political parties, expect the Nazi Party, and enjoyed unlimited power over the German state. A number of measures were taken to consolidate his power. The civil service, the judiciary and the professions were all purged of Hitler's political enemies and of Jews. Trade unions were also outlawed, giving workers no independent representation. The only institution within the state to retain independence was the army, which gradually found its power eroded by the growth of the SS, Hitler's personal bodyguard. The lack of any independent organisations within Nazi Germany makes it hard to assess the popularity of the regime and to measure the extent of opposition. Even so, it appears that Hitler's rule was popular and opposition to the regime was confined to a small minority in the army, in church groups and among former political opponents of the Nazi Party before 1933.

In spite of Hitler's unlimited constitutional power, the Nazi dictator hated government administration and allowed many decisions to be taken by Nazi ministers and numerous state, military and party institutions. As a result, some historians have claimed that Hitler's eccentric style of leadership made him a 'weak dictator', whose all-powerful status and alleged popularity were largely propaganda myths. Indeed, many historians now view Nazi Germany as a chaotic system of government with no clearly defined or co-ordinated decision-making process.

The projection of the Hitler myth over the German people was the task of the Ministry of Propaganda and Popular Enlightenment, under perhaps the most gifted propagandist of the twentieth century, Dr Joseph Goebbels, who aimed to control and manipulate the minds of the German people to support the Nazi regime. Under Goebbels, the Nazis did impose strict controls over the mass media, music, literature and the theatre. Goebbels very skilfully used the cinema to project Hitler as the popular and powerful leader of a happy and contented German people. Indeed, all the films we now see of Hitler in television documentaries are the carefully crafted work of Joseph Goebbels. He also manipulated the press to project the same image.

The Nazi regime attempted to impose its rigid beliefs on many aspects of German society. Those displaying any dissent or opposition faced imprisonment or were sent to concentration camps. These camps also contained gypsies, 'anti-social' elements and Jews. Over 30,000 communists were murdered by the Nazi regime, and 27,000 Germans were executed for 'high treason'.

The amalgamation of the civil police force with the SS created a form of legalised terror in which people were often arrested before they had actually done anything or because they were not viewed as likely to support the regime. The security forces also monitored public opinion, especially when the German armed forces began to suffer defeats on the battlefield in the latter stages of the Second World War.

Under Bernhard Rust, the minister of education, science and popular culture, universities and schools were encouraged to place less emphasis on traditional academic skills and concentrate more on practical life skills and the benefits of physical fitness. In schools, new textbooks were produced which fitted in with Nazi racial prejudices. Teachers were given detailed instructions about how subjects were to be taught. All pupils were given a history course on the rise of the Nazi Party, while, for example, biology and other science lessons emphasised Nazi ideas on race. Even exercises in mathematics were designed to fit in with Nazi racial and **eugenic** ideas.

The **eugenics** movement, established in Britain, the USA and parts of Europe, called for only healthy people to have children.

The Nazi regime also created a rival organisation to the formal school system – the Hitler Youth, which drilled young Germans in military disciplines and Nazi ideology. Members of the Hitler Youth were encouraged to recite Nazi slogans and to read poetry, usually praising the leadership qualities of Hitler.

At the heart of the German folk community under the Nazis was the family. The regime attempted to encourage marriage. New welfare benefits were offered to married couples with children. Young people were given advice on how to choose marriage partners. Each couple was given a loan at the outset of marriage which they did not have to repay if they produced four 'healthy' children. Women in Nazi Germany were expected to concentrate on being wives and mothers. Indeed, Hitler was very strongly opposed to ideas of female emancipation and equal rights for women. As a result, they were prohibited from taking public office and were barred from many professions. Abortion was also outlawed and birth control clinics closed down.

Another feature of life inside Nazi Germany was widespread anti-Semitism. Hitler had expressed a hatred of 'the Jews' throughout his political career. In his speeches, Jews were likened to 'vermin' and 'germs' which, by implication, had to be 'exterminated' before the goal of a 'racially pure' Germany could be created. Between 1933 and 1939, the Nazi regime introduced a range of anti-Semitic policies, beginning with legislation to remove civil and economic rights from Jews. The most openly violent act of anti-Semitism before 1939, within Nazi Germany, was *Kristallnacht* (the Night of Broken Glass), which took place on the evening of 9–10 November 1938. During a frenzied night of Nazi anti-Semitic violence, over 7,500 shops were destroyed, 400 Jewish synagogues were burned to the ground and approximately 90 Jews were murdered. Between 1939 and 1945, Nazi policies towards the Jews moved by stages to their mass extermination, which was carried out in Nazi-occupied Poland in a series of purpose-built death camps.

The criminal nature of the Nazi regime makes it difficult to evaluate whether Hitler did create a folk community. It remains difficult to separate the reality from the myth in assessing whether there was fundamental social change in Nazi Germany. There was opposition to the regime from groups within the army, the church, among communists and social democrats and even among youth. Even so, most Germans accepted there was no choice but to toe the party line.

Indeed, it is difficult to deny that Hitler was a popular leader. This was due not only to the skilful creation of the myth that he was an all-powerful and energetic leader, largely created by Goebbels, but also to the dramatic cut in unemployment, the upturn in the German economy and success in restoring Germany's status as a great power. Among many members of the middle classes and within old conservative circles the destruction of communist organisations and trade unions, strong law-and-order policies and the expansion of the armed forces were also warmly welcomed. Wide sections of the youth of Germany were also loyal to Hitler. As a consequence, it would be incorrect to suggest that Hitler's popularity was merely based on a combination of propaganda supported by terror. Above, all the 'Hitler myth' represented a desire for unity and harmony and the restoration of Germany as a great power. As Hitler moved from success to success in foreign policy from 1933 to 1941, his popularity soared, but once military defeat arrived in 1943, doubts began to creep in and even his most loyal supporters shared them. Even so, we must remember that Hitler remained popular right to the end of the war.

The aim of this chapter is to examine a wide range of contemporary documents on a number of different aspects of the domestic policies of the Nazi regime from 1933 to 1945.

Document study 1: How effectively did Hitler establish and consolidate Nazi authority?

1.1 The aims of the Nazis

The victory of the national socialist movement will mean the overcoming of the old class and caste spirit. It allows the nation once more to rise up out of status mania and class madness. It will train the nation to have an iron determination. It will overcome democracy. It will restore justice to the German people through the brutal assertion of the principle that no one has the right to hang the little ones so long as the biggest criminals go unpunished . . . National socialism fights for the German worker by getting him out of the hands of the swindlers and by destroying the protectors of international bank and stock exchange capital . . . With its victory the national socialist movement will protect the peasant through the ruthless education of our people to consume our own products . . . We want to ensure that in future the importance of our nation once again corresponds to its national worth.

Source: Nazi Party election manifesto, 1930, quoted in J. Noakes and G. Pridham, *Nazism 1919–1945, vol. 1: the rise to power 1919–1934*, University of Exeter Press, 1983, p. 72

1.2 The admission of Hitler to power, 1933

The notes of Joachim von Ribbentrop, a leading Nazi

Wednesday, 18th January . . . Hitler insists on being Chancellor. Papen considers this impossible. His influence with Hindenburg not strong enough to affect this. Hitler makes no further arrangements for talks.

Sunday 22nd January . . . Papen–Hitler talk. Papen will now press for Hitler as Chancellor but tells Hitler he will withdraw from these conversations if Hitler has no confidence in him.

Monday 23rd January . . . Papen saw Hindenburg who refused everything.

Friday 27th January . . . Hitler back in Berlin . . . New meeting with old Hindenburg arranged . . . In the evening I saw Papen and convinced him eventually that the only thing that made sense was Hitler's Chancellorship . . . Papen declared that . . . he was absolutely in favour of Hitler becoming Chancellor; this was the decisive change in Papen's attitude . . . Papen is now absolutely certain that he must achieve Hitler Chancellorship at all costs . . . This recognition by Papen is, I believe, the turning point. Papen has appointment with Hindenburg for Saturday at 10 a.m.

Saturday 28th January . . . About 11 a.m. I went to see Papen who received me with the question: 'Where is Hitler?' I told him that he had probably left, but could perhaps be contacted in Weimar. Papen said that he had to be got back [to Berlin] without delay, because a turning point had been reached; after a long talk with Hindenburg, he [Papen] considered Hitler's Chancellorship possible . . . Then we arranged a Papen–Hitler meeting for 11 a.m. Sunday morning.

Sunday 29th January . . . At 11 a.m. long Hitler–Papen talk. Hitler declared that on the whole everything was clear. But there would have to be general elections and an Enabling Law. Papen saw Hindenburg immediately. I lunched with Hitler . . . We discussed the elections. As Hindenburg does not want these, Hitler asked me to tell the President that these would be the last elections. In the afternoon . . . Papen declared that all obstacles were removed and that Hindenburg expects Hitler to-morrow at 11 a.m.

Monday 30th January: Hitler appointed Chancellor [after 11 a.m. meeting with Hindenburg].

Source: Notes by Joachim von Ribbentrop, presented at the Nuremberg trial of Nazi war criminals, 1946, quoted in J. Noakes and G. Pridham, *Nazism 1919–1945, vol. 1: the rise to power 1919–1934*, University of Exeter Press, 1983, pp. 118–20

1.3 Hitler's authority as Führer

1. At the head of the Reich stands the leader of the NSDAP [Hitler] as leader of the German Reich for life.
2. He is, on the strength of his being leader of the NSDAP, leader and Chancellor of the Reich. As such he embodies simultaneously Head of State, supreme state power and, as chief of the government, the central functions of the whole Reich administration. He is head of state and chief of government in one person. He is commander in chief of all the armed forces of the Reich.
3. The Führer is the constituent delegate of the German people, who without regard for formal pre-conditions decides the outward form of the Reich, its structure and general policy.
4. The Führer is the supreme judge of the nation . . . There is no position in the area of constitutional law in the Third Reich independent of this elemental will of the Führer.

Source: A German constitutionalist's view of the Third Reich, quoted in J. Noakes and G. Pridham, *Documents on Nazism, 1919–1945*, Jonathan Cape, 1974, p. 254

1.4 The projection of the Hitler myth in Nazi propaganda

The film . . . must capture in pictures the greatness of this day [Hitler's fifti-eth birthday] for all the future to see . . . the spirit of the hour must be cap-tured . . . and . . . the whole atmosphere of discipline and of concentrated power . . . Hitler receives the homage. The camera lingers lovingly on the Goebbels children all clothed in white, who stand curious but well behaved, next to Hitler, thus strengthening his reputation as a true lover of children – a special shot for women in the audience. Now the picture turns to the crowd. A gigantic chorus in front of the Reich swells in a song of jubilation for Hitler. Now Hitler appears on the balcony before the crowd, which breaks out in a repeated ovation.

Source: J. Noakes and G. Pridham, *Documents on Nazism, 1919–1945*, Jonathan Cape, 1974, p. 341

1.5 Hitler's style of leadership: the views of Albert Speer, a leading Nazi

When, I would often ask myself, did he really work? Little was left of the day; he rose late in the morning and conducted one or two conferences; but from the subsequent dinner on he more or less wasted his time . . . In the eyes of people Hitler was the Leader who watched over the nation day and night. This is hardly so. But Hitler's lax scheduling could be regarded as a life-style characteristic of the artistic temperament. According to my observations, he often allowed a problem to mature during the weeks when he seemed entirely taken up with trivial matters. Then after the 'sudden insight' came, he would spend a few days of intensive work giving final shape to his solu-tion . . . Once he had come to a decision, he relapsed again into his idleness.

Source: A. Speer, *Inside the Third Reich*, Sphere Books, 1970, p. 131

Document-study questions

1   From the evidence in 1.1 and your own knowledge, explain how the Nazi Party attempted to win electoral support.
2   What light does 1.2 shed on the negotiations which led to Hitler being made chancellor of Germany in 1933?
3   Offer an evaluation of Hitler's status within the Third Reich based on the information presented in 1.3.
4   What light does 1.4 shed on the projection of Hitler's image as an all-powerful leader in Nazi propaganda?
5   How reliable is 1.5 as evidence of Hitler's style of leadership?

Document study 2: What was the impact of Nazi policies on German society?

2.1 Control of political opponents by the SS–Gestapo police system

A message to Gestapo officers, April 1936

A list must be sent in by return of post of those people in your area who were prominent in opposing and slandering the National Socialist movement before the take-over of power. The following details are requested . . . The first name and surname, the date and place of birth, whether or not a Jew, present domicile, profession, including all offices held by the person concerned, whether in receipt of a pension etc. And whether the person had his citizenship revoked . . . Furthermore, his present occupation must be reported. At the same time, a detailed report must be made about incidents in which the individual was involved, particularly hostile activity towards the NSDAP [Nazi Party], and whether the person in question is still a clandestine opponent of the National Socialist State or has drawn attention to himself by acting in a hostile way towards the State and the Party.

Source: J. Noakes and G. Pridham, *Nazism 1919–1945, vol. 2: state, economy and society 1933–1939*, University of Exeter Press, 1984, pp. 517–18

2.2 Dr Joseph Goebbels on the aims of Nazi propaganda

The most important tasks of this Ministry must be the following. Firstly, all propaganda ventures and all institutions for the enlightenment of the people . . . must be centralized in one hand. Furthermore, it must be our task to instil into these propaganda activities a modern feeling . . . Technology must not be allowed to proceed ahead of the Reich; the Reich must go along with technology. We are living now in an age when the masses must support policies . . . It is the task of State propaganda so to simplify complicated ways of thinking that even the smallest man in the street may understand.

Source: J. Noakes and G. Pridham, *Documents on Nazism, 1919–1945*, Jonathan Cape, 1974, p. 334

Joseph Goebbels (1897–1945).

2.3 The role of the universities

The university is not only the place of research, but also the place of education. We cannot measure the value of a German university only by the number of academic publications; we must consider it from another standpoint. Gentlemen, during those years when this un-German state and its un-German leadership barred the way to German youth, you, in your professional solitude and devotion to your great work of research, overlooked the fact that youth looked to you to lead the future of the German nation. Youth was marching while you, gentlemen, were not out in front.

Source: J. Noakes and G. Pridham, *Documents on Nazism, 1919–1945*, Jonathan Cape, 1974, p. 341

2.4 Mathematics under the Nazis

1. The construction of a lunatic asylum costs 6 million RM. [Reichsmark]. How many houses at 15,000 RM. could have been built for that amount?

Source: J. Laver, *Nazi Germany: documents at source*, Hodder and Stoughton, 1991, p. 44

2.5 'Vow'. A poem of the Hitler Youth

You, Führer, are our commander!
We stand in your name.
The Reich is the object of our struggle.
It is the beginning and the Amen.

Your word is the heartbeat of our deeds.
Your faith builds cathedrals for us.
And even when death reaps the last harvest.
The crowd of the Reich never fails.

We are ready, your silent spell
Welds our ranks like iron.
Like a chain, man beside man,
Into a wall of loyalty round you.

You, Führer, are our commander!
We stand in your name.
The Reich is the object of our struggle,
It is the beginning and the Amen.

Source: J. Noakes and G. Pridham, *Documents on Nazism, 1919–1945*, Jonathan Cape, 1974, p. 358

2.6 Rules for marriage

Instructions to women in choosing a marriage partner

1. Remember that you are a German.
2. If you are genetically healthy you should not remain unmarried.
3. Keep your body pure.
4. You should keep your mind and spirit pure.
5. As a German choose only a spouse of the same Nordic blood.
6. In choosing a spouse, ask about his ancestors.
7. Health is also a precondition for physical beauty.
8. Marry only for love.
9. Don't look for a playmate but for a companion for marriage.
10. You should want to have as many children as possible.

Source: 'The Ten Commandments of a spouse', Berlin, 1934

2.7 Hitler's views on the role of women in Nazi Germany

If the man's world is said to be the state, his struggle, his readiness to devote his powers to the service of the community, then it may perhaps be said that the woman's world is a smaller world. For her world is her husband, her family, her children, and her home. But what would become of the greater world if there was no one to tend and care for the smaller one . . . Providence has entrusted to the woman the cares of that world which is her very own, and only on the basis of this smaller world can the man's world be formed and built up. The two worlds are not antagonistic. They complement each other . . . We do not consider it correct for the woman to interfere in the world of the man.

Source: *Frankfurter Zeitung*, 9 September 1934

Document-study questions

1 How useful is 2.1, written by a member of the Gestapo in 1936, for explaining how the Nazi police system dealt with political opponents?
2 In 2.2, what does Goebbels view as the key aims of Nazi propaganda?
3 What does 2.3 reveal about the Nazi attitude towards a university education?
4 What does 2.4 indicate about the Nazi attitude towards the mentally ill?
5 From the evidence in 2.5 and your own knowledge, explain how the Hitler Youth attempted to support the ideas of the Nazi regime.
6 What light does 2.6 shed on the role of marriage within Nazi society?
7 How does Hitler see the role of women in Nazi society, as outlined in 2.7?

Document study 3: How did the Nazis deal with the 'Jewish question'?

3.1 The Nuremberg Laws 1

The Law for the Protection of German Blood, 15 September 1935

Entirely convinced that the purity of German blood is essential to the further existence of the German people, and inspired by the uncompromising determination to safeguard the future of the German nation, the Reichstag has unanimously adopted the following law . . . Marriages between Jews and citizens of German or kindred blood are forbidden. Marriages concluded in defiance of this law are void, even if, for the purpose of evading the law, they were concluded abroad . . . Sexual relations outside marriage between Jews and nationals of German or kindred blood are forbidden . . . Jews will not be permitted to employ female citizens of German or kindred blood under 45 years of age as domestic servants . . . Jews are forbidden to display the Reich and national flag . . . On the other hand they are permitted to display the Jewish colours [Star of David].

Source: J. Noakes and G. Pridham, *Nazism 1919–1945, vol. 2: state, economy and society 1933–1939*, University of Exeter Press, 1984, pp. 535–36

3.2 The Nuremberg Laws 2

Reich Citizenship Law, 15 September 1935

A subject of the Reich is that subject only who is of German or kindred blood and who, through his conduct, shows that he is both desirous and fit to serve the German people and Reich faithfully . . . The right to citizenship is acquired by the granting of Reich citizenship papers . . . Only the citizen of the Reich enjoys full political rights in accordance with the provision of the laws . . . A Jew cannot be a citizen of the Reich. He has no right to vote in political affairs and he cannot occupy public office.

Source: J. Noakes and G. Pridham, *Nazism 1919–1945, vol. 2: state, economy and society 1933–1939*, University of Exeter Press, 1984, pp. 536–39

3.3 The Nuremberg Laws 3

The legal definition of a Jew

A Jew is anyone who is descended from at least three grandparents who are racially full Jews . . . A Jew is also one who is descended from two full Jewish grandparents, if (a) he belonged to the Jewish religious community at the time the law was issued or joins the community later, (b) he was married to a Jewish person, at the time the law was issued, or marries one subsequently, (c) he is the offspring of a marriage with a Jew . . . (d) he is the offspring of an extramarital relationship with a Jew . . . The Führer and Reich Chancellor can grant exemptions from the regulations laid down in the law.

Source: J. Noakes and G. Pridham, *Nazism 1919–1945, vol. 2: state, economy and society 1933–1939*, University of Exeter Press, 1984, pp. 536–39

3.4 A Hitler Youth member's views of *Kristallnacht*

I went into Berlin very early [the morning after *Kristallnacht*] to go to the Reich Youth Leadership office. I noticed nothing unusual on the way. I alighted at the Alexanderplatz. In order to get to the Lothringerstrasse I had to go down a rather gloomy alley containing many small shops and inns. To my surprise almost all the shop windows here were smashed in. The pavement was covered with pieces of glass and fragments of broken furniture . . . For the space of a second I was clearly aware that something terrible had happened there. Something frightfully brutal. But almost at once I switched over to accepting what had happened as over and done with and avoiding critical reflection, I said to myself: The Jews are the enemies of the new Germany. Last night they had a taste of what this means. Let us hope that World Jewry, which has resolved to hinder Germany's 'new steps towards greatness', will take the events of last night as a warning . . . With these and similar thoughts I constructed for myself a justification for the pogrom. But in any case I forced the memory of it out of my consciousness as quickly as possible. As the years went by, I grew better and better at switching off quickly in this manner on similar occasions. It was the only way, whatever the circumstances, to prevent the onset of doubts about the rightness of what had happened.

Source: J. Noakes and G. Pridham, *Documents on Nazism, 1919–1945*, Jonathan Cape, 1974, p. 476

3.5 Hitler orders the 'Final Solution'

The evidence of Rudolf Hoess, camp commandant of Auschwitz, given at the Nuremberg trial of Nazi war criminals, 1946

In the summer of 1941, I cannot remember the exact date, I was suddenly summoned to the Reichsführer SS [Heinrich Himmler], directly by his adjunct's office. Contrary to his usual caution, Himmler received me without his adjutant being present and said to me in effect 'The Führer has ordered that the Jewish Question be solved once and for all and we, the SS, are to implement that order. The existing extermination centres in the east are not in a position to carry out the large actions which are anticipated. I have, therefore, earmarked Auschwitz for this purpose.'

Source: J. Noakes and G. Pridham, *Nazism 1919–1945, vol. 3: foreign policy, war and racial extermination*, University of Exeter Press, pp. 1105–06

Document-study questions

1 From the evidence in 3.1, can you outline the major terms of the Law for the Protection of German Blood?

2 What evidence does 3.2 offer of the legal status of a Jew under the Nazis?

3 Give a clear definition of what constitutes a 'Jew', under the Nuremberg Laws, from the evidence contained in 3.3.

4 What light does 3.4 shed on how some Nazi supporters reacted to openly violent displays of anti-Semitism within Germany?

5 How reliable is 3.5 in explaining Hitler's role in ordering the 'Final Solution' of the 'Jewish question'?

Document study 4: What impact did Nazi economic policies have on Germany in the 1930s?

4.1 Unemployment in Germany, 1932–39

Year (July)	1932	1933	1934	1935	1936	1937	1938	1939
Millions unemployed	5.392	4.464	2.426	1.754	1.170	0.536	0.218	0.038

Source: D. G. Williamson, *The Third Reich*, Longman, 1992, *passim*

4.2 Hitler on the Four Year Plan, 1936

Germany's economic situation is . . . in the briefest outline as follows.

. . . We are over-populated and cannot feed ourselves from our own resources . . . When the nation has six or seven million unemployed, the food situation improves because these people lack purchasing power. It naturally makes a difference whether six million people have 40 marks a month to spend, or 100 marks . . . This means an increased and understandable run on the foodstuffs market . . . We lack foodstuffs and basic raw materials . . . The final solution lies in extending our living space, that it to say, extending the sources of raw materials and food stuffs. It is the task of the political leadership one day to solve this problem.

. . . I thus set the following tasks

i. The German armed forces must be operational within four years

ii. The German economy must be fit for war in four years

Source: J. Noakes and G. Pridham, *Documents on Nazism, 1919–1945*, Jonathan Cape, 1974, pp. 401–08

4.3 A left-wing view of Nazi economic policies

A satirical montage mocking the words of Göring's speech of 1935: 'Ore has always made an empire strong, butter and lard have only served to make its people fat.'

Source: John Heartfield, 'Hooray, the butter is gone!', 1935

Document-study questions

1   What does 4.1 tell us about how successfully the Nazi regime dealt with the problem of unemployment?
2   What light does 4.2 shed on the link between the economic policy of the Nazi regime and its foreign policy objectives?
3   Compare the view of the Four Year Plan given in 4.2 with the one presented of Nazi economics in 4.3.

Document study 5: What was the impact of the war on the popularity of Hitler and the Nazi regime?

5.1 The reaction of the German public to defeat at Stalingrad

A report from the Security Police (SD), 28 January 1943

At the moment the whole nation is deeply shaken by the impression that the fate of the Sixth Army [at Stalingrad] is sealed and by concern about the further development of the war situation. Among the many questions arising from the changed situation, people ask above all why Stalingrad was not evacuated or relieved and how it was possible, only a few months ago, to describe the military situation as secure and as not unfavourable. In particular, people discuss, with a marked undertone of criticism, the underestimation of the Russian combat forces . . . Fearing that an unfavourable end to the war is now possible, many compatriots are seriously thinking about the consequences of defeat. While some people say that 'perhaps it would not be so bad', most people are convinced that losing the war will amount to extinction.

Source: J. Noakes and G. Pridham, *Nazism 1919–1945, vol. 4: the German home front in World War II*, University of Exeter Press, 1998, p. 543

5.2 The views of the German people towards Hitler after the defeat of German forces at the Battle of Stalingrad

A summary of reports of local Nazi representatives prepared by the party chancellery, March 1943

. . . People are now daring openly to criticize the Führer and to attack him in the most mean and spiteful manner. These following rumours and political jokes have been reported . . . The clock goes tick tack and the hand goes forward; Rommel goes backward . . . The Führer is mentally disturbed and is tearing down pictures and curtains in his headquarters . . . These political jokes are all too readily listened to by a certain group of compatriots. Unfortunately, inspired by a certain sensationalism, boastfulness or indifference many compatriots repeat everything which they are told without contradiction and without bearing in mind that in doing so they are becoming channels of enemy propaganda. It is a regrettable fact, which one is constantly being made aware of, that our party comrades frequently display an incredible doziness and thoughtlessness since they no doubt witness such demoralizing enemy propaganda and yet rarely show the courage needed to crack down on this.

Source: J. Noakes and G. Pridham, *Nazism 1919–1945, vol. 4: the German home front in World War II*, University of Exeter Press, 1998, p. 549

5.3 Public opinion as Germany faces defeat in the Second World War

A report from the Security Police (SD), 30 March 1944

The news of the deterioration on the eastern front, the unchanged situation in the air war, the lack of any sign of a counter blow from us or of an enemy invasion, which would release general tension, together with the day-to-day problems caused by the war – all these sustain a downbeat mood among the population. At the moment, large sections of the population are intimidated by the military situation. People do not know what they should believe. Even compatriots who have hitherto been loyal are finding that 'the situation is gradually getting worrying' . . . The majority of compatriots hold to the belief that whatever happens they have to keep going and 'grit their teeth'. One does it because one has to and 'because there is no alternative left'.

Source: J. Noakes and G. Pridham, *Nazism 1919–1945, vol. 4: the German home front in World War II*, University of Exeter Press, 1998, p. 577

Document-study questions

1   How useful is 5.1 for explaining the morale of the German people after the Battle of Stalingrad?
2   What does the evidence in 5.2 reveal about the extent to which the German people believed the Hitler myth?
3   How useful is 5.3, written by a member of the Nazi Security Police, for explaining the state of German morale towards the end of the Second World War?

Document study 6: What was the nature of the resistance to the Nazi regime?

6.1 Communist resistance

Underground leaflet produced by communists, 1941

Germany is in peril. It is a peril from within. If a ship is in distress, people throw everything overboard which can threaten them. So everything which can harm the nation must now be removed from its midst . . . Hitler is not the State, we are the State, we are the people! The people must now form themselves into battalions . . . they must march together as a national front for a free and independent Germany.

Source: J. Noakes and G. Pridham, *Nazism 1919–1945, vol. 4: the German home front in World War II*, University of Exeter Press, 1998, p. 585

6.2 The bomb plot against Hitler, 20 July 1944

The proclamation which was to be issued by Colonel Beck to the German people by the new government in the event of Hitler's death, July 1944

Germans! Hitler's dictatorship has been destroyed. In the last few years monstrous things have been going on before our eyes. Hitler, who was not summoned by the German people but arrived at the pinnacle of government through the worst sort of intrigues, through demonic arts and lies, through the incredible wastage of resources, which appeared to bring advantages to everybody but in reality plunged us into debt and shortages, confused the minds and spirit of our people and even produced fatal illusions outside Germany. In order to maintain himself in power he established a reign of terror . . . Numerous Germans but also members of other nations have been languishing in concentration camps for years exposed to the worst kinds of torture and often subjected to terrible torturers. Many of them have died. Our good name has been besmirched by cruel mass murder. With his hands steeped in blood, Hitler has followed his tortuous path leaving tears, suffering and misery in his wake. His insane contempt for all human feelings has with deadly certainty plunged our nation into ruins, his claim to military genius has led our brave soldiers to disaster . . . Our aim is to achieve the community of the people based on respect, helpfulness and social justice. We want . . . the rule of law and freedom to replace force and terror, truth and probity to replace lies and selfishness. We want to restore our honour and thus our respect in the community of nations . . . We see a just peace, which instead of the nations fighting and destroying each other will ensure peaceful co-operation.

Source: J. Noakes and G. Pridham, *Nazism 1919–1945, vol. 4: the German home front in World War II*, University of Exeter Press, 1998, pp. 619–20

Document-study questions

1 How useful is 6.1 for explaining the aims of communist opponents of the Nazi regime?
2 How useful is 6.2, written by a leading member of the bomb plot against Hitler in July 1944, for explaining the kind of regime which might have been introduced had Hitler been killed?

Further reading

Russia: the road to revolution, 1890–1917

The following books all provide very useful information on the road to the Russian Revolution: E. Acton, *Rethinking the Russian Revolution* (Edward Arnold, 1990); R. Service, *The Russian Revolution 1900–1927* (Macmillan, 1986); J. White, *A short history of the Russian Revolution* (Edward Arnold, 1994); and A. Wood, *The origins of the Russian Revolution* (Methuen, 1987).

A good survey of the social and economic causes of the Revolution can be found in M. Ferro, *The Bolshevik Revolution* (Routledge and Kegan Paul, 1985). For Lenin's role see A. Ulam, *Lenin and the Bolsheviks* (Fontana, 1969).

The origins of the First World War, 1890–1914

The following books all provide very good introductions to the origins of the First World War: R. Henig, *The origins of the First World War* (Routledge, 1989); J. Joll, *The origins of the First World War* (Longman, 1984); G. Martel, *The origins of the First World War* (second edition, Longman, 1995); and F. McDonough, *The origins of the First and Second World Wars* (Cambridge University Press, 1997).

The First World War and its consequences

Most of the books written on the First World War tend to be long and often specialised studies, most notably B. Liddel Hart's *The history of the First World War* (Pan, 1972). However, a very good, student-friendly introduction is provided by A. Marwick, *World War I* (Open University Press, 1973), which contains a good set of documents. Another useful study is K. Robbins, *The First World War* (Oxford University Press, 1984). For the civilian experience of war see J. Winter, *The experience of World War I* (Edinburgh University Press, 1988). It must be said that there are hardly any shorter books on the First World War, and very little in the way of a stimulating historical debate to match the very extensive literature on the origins of the war.

The Paris peace settlement and its aftermath, 1919–33

There are a number of good books on the Paris peace settlement and its aftermath, most notably: A. Adamthwaite, *The lost peace: international relations in Europe*

1918–1939 (Edward Arnold, 1980); R. Henig, *The League of Nations* (Edinburgh University Press, 1973); R. Henig, *Versailles and after, 1919–1933* (second edition, Routledge, 1995); R. A. C. Parker, *Europe 1919–1945* (Weidenfeld and Nicholson, 1969); and G. Ross, *The great powers and the decline of the European states system 1914–1945* (Longman, 1983).

Italy, 1919–45: the rise and fall of Mussolini and fascism

The following books provide useful information on the rise and fall of fascism in Italy: M. Blinkhorn, *Mussolini and Fascist Italy* (Routledge, 1994); M. Clark, *Modern Italy* (Longman, 1984); R. Griffin, *The nature of Fascism* (Routledge, 1993); J. Hite and C. Hintin, *Fascist Italy* (John Murray, 1998); and S. Lee, *European dictatorships* (Routledge, 1987).

Germany, 1918–45: the rise and fall of the Third Reich

There are many very good books on the rise and fall of the Weimar Republic and the rise of Hitler, including: E. Fuechtwanger, *From Weimar to Hitler* (Macmillan, 1993); C. Fisher, *The rise of the Nazis* (Manchester University Press, 1995); R. Henig, *The Weimar Republic* (Routledge, 1998); M. Kater, *The Nazi Party* (Blackwell, 1983); E. Kolb, *The Weimar Republic* (Unwin Hyman, 1988); and A. J. Nicholls, *Weimar and the rise of Hitler* (Macmillan, 1992).

There are numerous books on Hitler and Nazi Germany, and Cambridge University Press has two of them in a student-friendly form: F. McDonough, *Hitler and Nazi Germany* (1999) and W. Simpson, *Hitler and Germany* (1991).

Other useful books for 'A' level include: R. Harvey, *Hitler and the Third Reich* (Stanley Thornes, 1998); L. Rees, *The Nazis: a warning from history* (BBC Books, 1997); and D. G. Williamson, *The Third Reich* (Longman, 1982). For a brilliant study of the historical debate see I. Kershaw, *The Hitler myth: image and reality in the Third Reich* (Oxford University Press, 1989). However, this book will probably be more useful to you if you intend to study Nazi Germany at university.

The origins of the Second World War

There is a vast literature on the origins of the Second World War. The following provide good introductions to both the subject and the historical debate: P. M. H. Bell, *The origins of the Second World War in Europe* (Longman, 1986); R. Henig, *The origins of the Second World War* (Routledge, 1985); F. McDonough, *The origins of the First and Second World Wars* (Cambridge University Press, 1997); and A. J. P. Taylor *The origins of the Second World War* (Hamish Hamilton, 1961).

Index